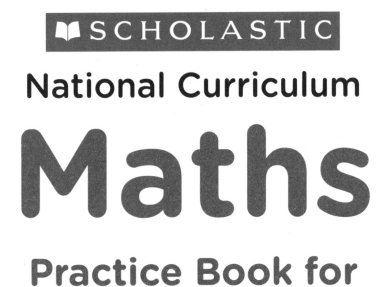

SCHOLASTIC

National Curriculum
Maths
Practice Book for

Year 2

D0230891

Book End, Range Road, Witney, Oxfordshire, OX29 0YD
www.scholastic.co.uk

© 2014, Scholastic Ltd

14 15 16 17 18 19   4 5 6 7 8 9 0 1 2 3

British Library Cataloguing-in-Publication Data
A catalogue record for this book is available from the British Library.

ISBN 978-1407-12889-4
Printed by Bell and Bain Ltd, Glasgow

Editorial
Rachel Morgan, Robin Hunt, Kate Baxter, Lesley Fletcher, Sara Wiegand

Design
Scholastic Design Team: Neil Salt, Nicolle Thomas
and Oxford Designers & Illustrators Ltd

Cover Design
Neil Salt

Illustration
Cathy Hughes

Contents

Why buy this book?

The *100 Practice Activities* series has been designed to support the National Curriculum in schools in England. The curriculum is challenging in mathematics and includes the requirement for children's understanding to be secure before moving on. These practice books will help your child revise and practise all of the skills they will learn at school, including some topics they might not have encountered previously.

How to use this book

- The content is divided into National Curriculum topics (for example, Addition and subtraction, Fractions and so on). Find out what your child is doing in school and dip into the relevant practice activities as required. The index at the back of the book will help you to identify appropriate topics.

- Share the activities and support your child if necessary using the helpful quick tips at the top of most pages.

- Keep the working time short and come back to an activity if your child finds it too difficult. Ask your child to note any areas of difficulty at the back of the book. Don't worry if your child does not 'get' a concept first time, as children learn at different rates and content is likely to be covered throughout the school year.

- Check your child's answers using the answers section on www.scholastic.co.uk/100practice/mathsy2 where you will also find additional interactive activities for your child to play, and some extra resources to support your child's learning (such as number grids and a times tables chart).

- Give lots of encouragement and tick off the progress chart as your child completes each chapter.

How to use the book

This tells you which topic you're working on.

This is the title of the activity.

These boxes will help you with the activity.
(If there's not one on your page, go back and find the last one.)

This is the instruction text. It tells you what to do.

Arrow sentences

Choose two numbers from the boxes and make an arrow sentence.
One example has been done for you, using the numbers 12 and 6.

+ 6	12 + 6 = 18
12 18	
– 6	18 – 6 = 12

+	+	=
–	–	=

+	+	=
–	–	=

+	+	=
–	–	=

+	+	=
–	–	=

2	3	4	5	6	7	8	9	10
11	12	13	14	15	16	17		

Missing numbers

Finding missing numbers can be tricky. You can use cubes or a pencil and paper to 'work out' the problem.
Remember to use the inverse operation.

☐ – 17 = 8, then 17 + 8 = 25.

You will then find the missing number (25). 25 – 17 = 8.

Magic Mark has made some of the numbers disappear.
Put the correct numbers back in to the number sentences.

a. 26 – 12 = ◯   **b.** 31 – ◯ = 13

c. ◯ – 23 = 14   **d.** ◯ – 20 = 24

e. 36 – ◯ = 24   **f.** 17 – ◯ = 13

g. 29 – 17 = ◯

h. ◯ – 37 = 11

Monster multiplication

Read each problem. Think how many equal groups there are:

3 + 3 + 3 or 3 × 3.

There are nine eyes altogether.

Write a multiplication number sentence for each group of monsters.

5 monsters with 2 eyes each
2 monsters with 7 eyes each
10 monsters with 3 eyes each
5 monsters with 4 eyes each
6 monsters with 10 eyes each
10 monsters with 5 eyes each
5 monsters with 8 eyes each

Multiplication facts

To work out ☐ × 10m = 30m ask: How many 10s are there in 30?

Division will help you: 30 ÷ 10. The missing number is 3.
Work out each fact and solve the problem:

1. Fill in the missing amounts.

a. 2 × 10kg = ☐ kg   **b.** 6 × ☐ p = 12p

c. ☐ × 5cm = 35cm   **d.** 4 × ☐ m = 40m

e. 8p × 2 = ☐ p   **f.** ☐ × 5g = 50g

2. Answer these questions.

a. Nine groups of five. How many altogether? ☐

b. Seven times two equals? ☐

3. Complete the grid.

×	0	1	2	3	4	5	6	7	8	9	10
2										18	
10						50					

Follow the instruction to complete the activity.

You might have to write on lines, in boxes, draw or circle things.

If you need help, ask an adult!

Hopscotch counting

To work out the missing numbers, ask: What steps are you counting in?

Tip: If you are counting in 10s, the 1s digit stays the same: 12, 22, 32, 42...

Fill in the missing numbers on these hopscotch frames.

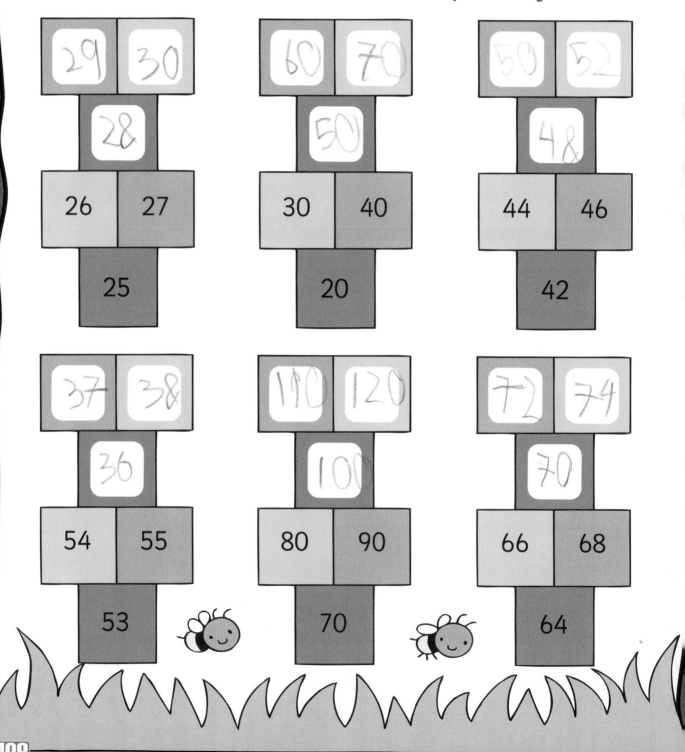

Counting on and back

The first number below gives you the rule to follow for each pattern.
You will need to count on or count back from the starting number.

Write the missing numbers. The first one is done for you.

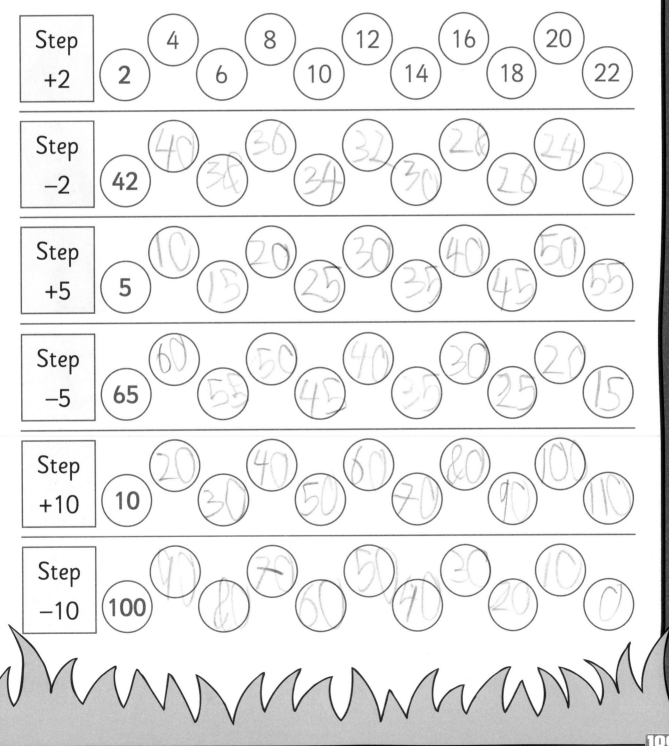

| Step +2 | 2 | 4 | 6 | 8 | 10 | 12 | 14 | 16 | 18 | 20 | 22 |

Step −2: 42, 40, 38, 36, 34, 32, 30, 28, 26, 24, 22

Step +5: 5, 10, 15, 20, 25, 30, 35, 40, 45, 50, 55

Step −5: 65, 60, 55, 50, 45, 40, 35, 30, 25, 20, 15

Step +10: 10, 20, 30, 40, 50, 60, 70, 80, 90, 100, 110

Step −10: 100, 90, 80, 70, 60, 50, 40, 30, 20, 10, 0

Snakes and ladders counting

Do the numbers below count up or down?
Next, try to work out the difference between the numbers.
Finally, put the first number in your head and count on or
back to work out the next number.

Complete these number sequences and then make up
some of your own.

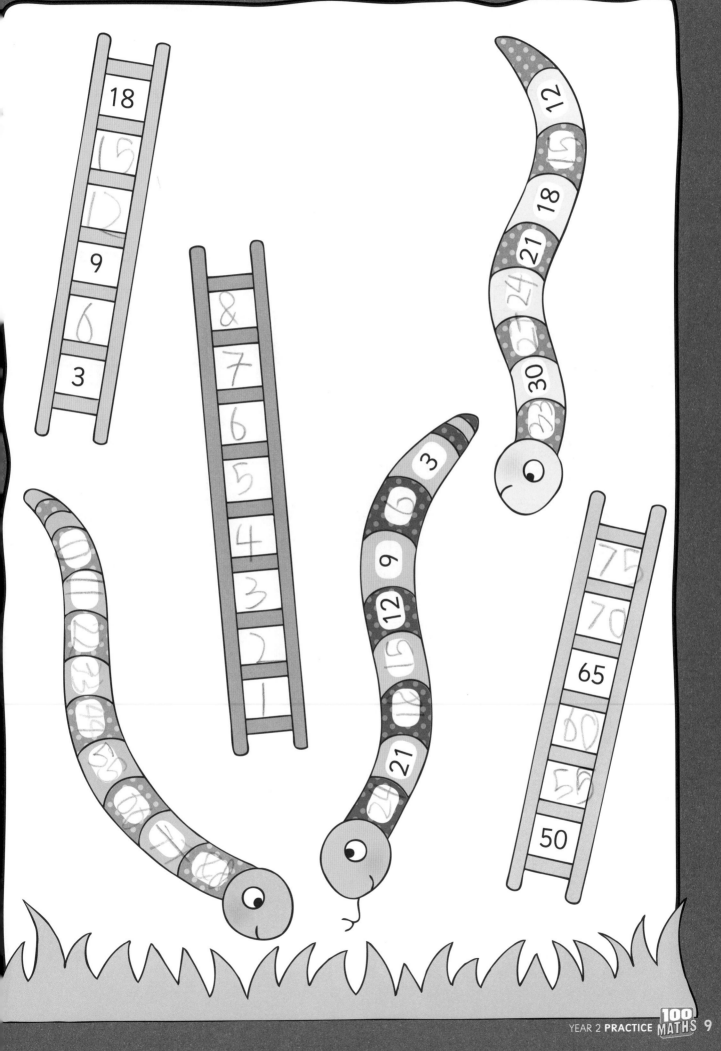

Hopscotch 10s

Practise counting on or back in 10s from different 1- and 2-digit numbers.

What do you notice about the 10s digits each time?

What do you notice about the 1s digit each time?

Fill in the missing numbers on these hopscotch frames.

Counting and grouping

Grouping numbers helps you to count easily.
Try marking each dot as you count it, and then draw a circle to group them.
Write the number of dots in each group to help you to add them.

Count these dots by drawing around each group of 10.

How many dots are there?

Count these dots by drawing around each group of 5.

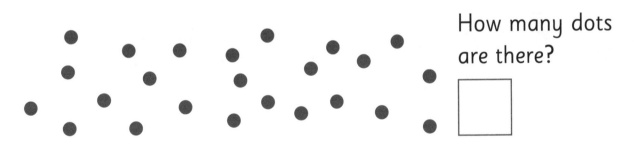

How many dots are there?

Count these dots by drawing around each group of 2.

How many dots are there?

Count them up!

Count the jellybeans in 2s.

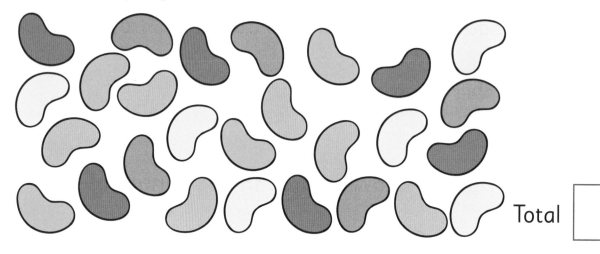

Total ☐

Count the soldiers in 5s.

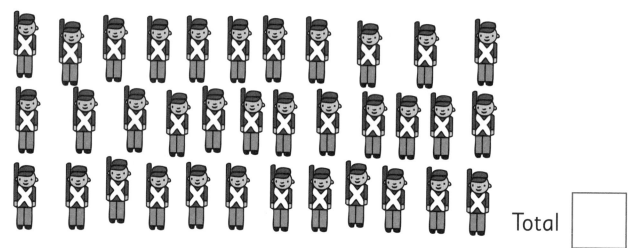

Total ☐

Count the balloons in 10s.

Total ☐

Patterns on a 100 square

The patterns on a 100 square can help when you add, subtract or multiply.

Count in 2s, starting at 2. Colour these numbers red.
Count in 3s, starting at 3. Colour these numbers blue.
Count in 5s, starting at 5. Colour these numbers green.
Look at all the number patterns you have made.

Which numbers are in all three patterns? _____

1	2	3	4	5	6	7	8	9	10
11	12	13	14	15	16	17	18	19	20
21	22	23	24	25	26	27	28	29	30
31	32	33	34	35	36	37	38	39	40
41	42	43	44	45	46	47	48	49	50
51	52	53	54	55	56	57	58	59	60
61	62	63	64	65	66	67	68	69	70
71	72	73	74	75	76	77	78	79	80
81	82	83	84	85	86	87	88	89	90
91	92	93	94	95	96	97	98	99	100

Combining 10s and 1s

2-digit numbers are made up by combining 10s and 1s:
28 = 20 + 8.

Put the 10s and 1s cards together to make 16 new numbers. Record each sum. One has been done for you:

40 + 1 = 41

Place value grid

With the number **163**, work out:
How many 100s are in that number?
How many 10s? How many 1s?

100s	10s	1s
1	6	3

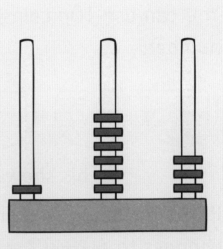

This will help you with additions and subtractions.

Partition these numbers into 100s, 10s and 1s. Write them in the correct column in the table.

	100s	10s	1s
seventy-eight			
forty-seven			
one hundred and twenty-three			
one hundred and four			

Partitioning 2-digit numbers

You can use 10p coins and 1p coins to make a 2-digit number.

This shows the addition 50 + 2 = 52.

If you move a 10p coin towards the 1p coins the addition changes to 40 + 12 = 52. Keep moving the 10p coins towards the 1p coins (one at a time) to find more additions.

1. Split these 2-digit numbers into 10s and 1s to make an addition.

32   _____ + _____ = _____

47   _____ + _____ = _____

81   _____ + _____ = _____

65   _____ + _____ = _____

2. Can you find all the additions for 74?

_____

_____

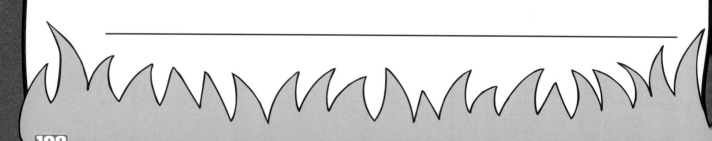

3. Work out the total for these additions. Write two other additions for each.

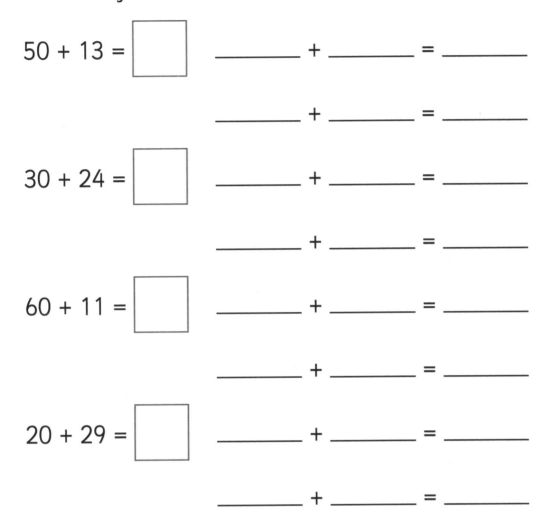

50 + 13 = ☐   _____ + _____ = _____

_____ + _____ = _____

30 + 24 = ☐   _____ + _____ = _____

_____ + _____ = _____

60 + 11 = ☐   _____ + _____ = _____

_____ + _____ = _____

20 + 29 = ☐   _____ + _____ = _____

_____ + _____ = _____

4. Choose your own 2-digit number. Work out three additions.

_____

_____

_____

Ordering and drawing numbers

Before drawing a 2-digit number on an abacus, decide which number is the 10s and which is the 1s:

two 10s ➡ 27 ⬅ seven 1s

Tip: To order numbers, start with the lowest 10s number, and then look for the next lowest 10s number.

Order these numbers from lowest to highest. Write them in the small boxes below.

89   45   57   23   94   69   ~~17~~   38   70

Draw an abacus picture to match each number.

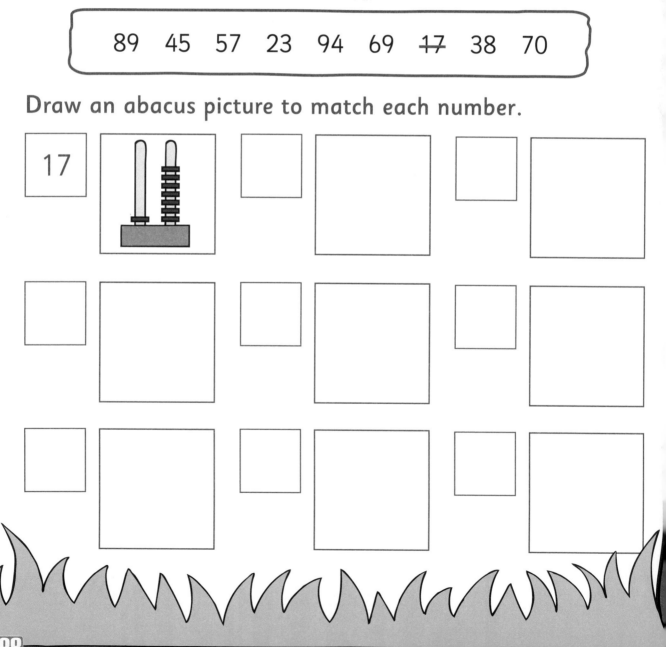

17

Comparing and ordering numbers

Look at the 10s number to help you order numbers.
For **5**4 and **3**7, 37 has fewer 10s than 54, so is the lower number.
If the 10s numbers are the same, look at the 1s.
For **3**5 and **3**7, 35 has five 1s, so is lower than 37.

1. Help Charlie arrange these chairs in the correct order – lowest number first.

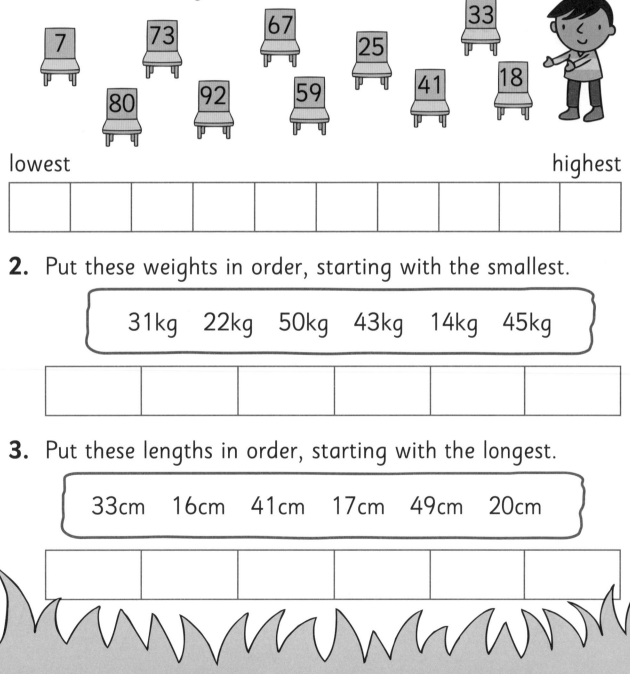

lowest   highest

2. Put these weights in order, starting with the smallest.

31kg   22kg   50kg   43kg   14kg   45kg

3. Put these lengths in order, starting with the longest.

33cm   16cm   41cm   17cm   49cm   20cm

Using <, > and =

< means **less than**   15 < 20.
> means **greater than**   20 > 15.
Tip: The open part of the sign always faces the bigger number.
= means **the same as** or **equals**: 5 = 5.

Fill in the missing sign: <, > or =.

1. 23 ☐ 42

2. 17 ☐ 9

3. 37 ☐ 18

4. 72 ☐ 89

5. 7 + 3 ☐ 6 + 4

6. 27 + 6 ☐ 32 − 4

7. 45 − 6 ☐ 30 + 9

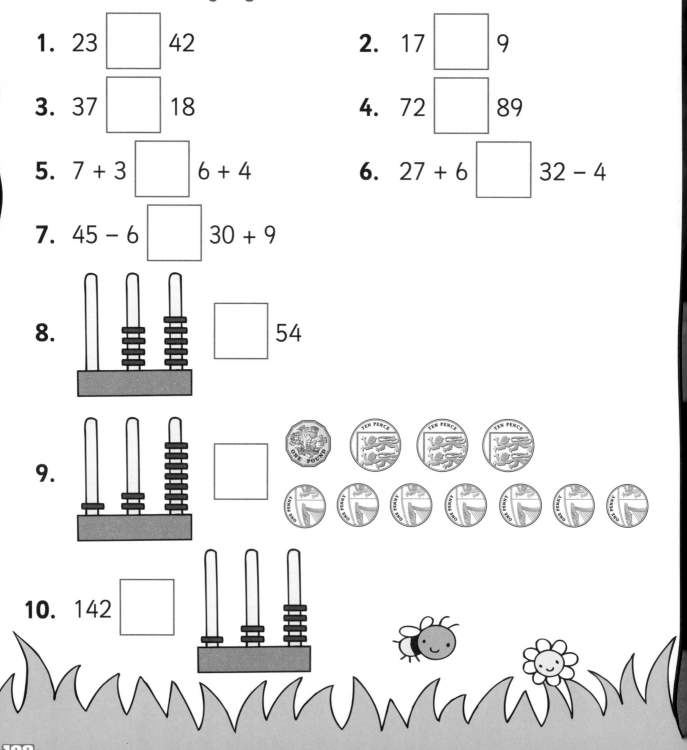

8. ☐ 54

9.

10. 142 ☐

Are these true or false? Tick the correct box.

	True	False
1. 22 > 24	☐	☐
2. 42 < 43	☐	☐
3. 63 > 77	☐	☐
4. 92 < 89	☐	☐

Write the correct sign: < or >.

1.

2.

3.

Number lines and number grids

Working out number patterns is like cracking a code. First, check if the numbers are counting up or down. Next, find the difference between the numbers.

| 51 | 49 | | | 43 |

Here the numbers are counting down in 2s.

1. Fill in the missing numbers on the snakes.

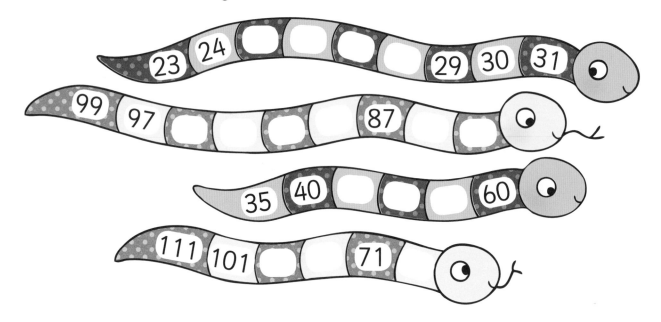

2. Fill in the missing measurements.

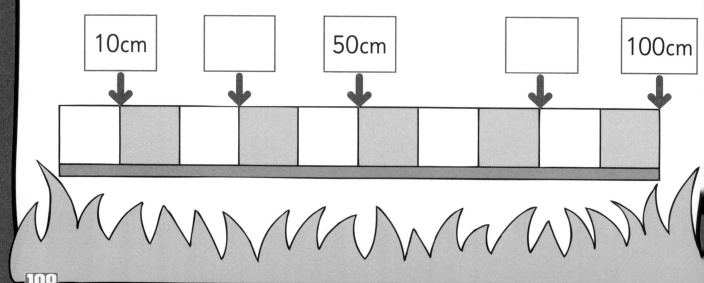

3. Complete these missing-number grids.

2		
		10

5	10	
	40	

	101	
103	104	

41		45
		51
		57

	12	15
18		

	31	29
	19	

Estimating numbers on a number line

To estimate, think where halfway would be.
Where would 1 be? Where would 10 be?

0   20

Halfway is 10. The bear is just before 10. So it is on 9.

Look at each number line. Work out which number each animal is standing on.

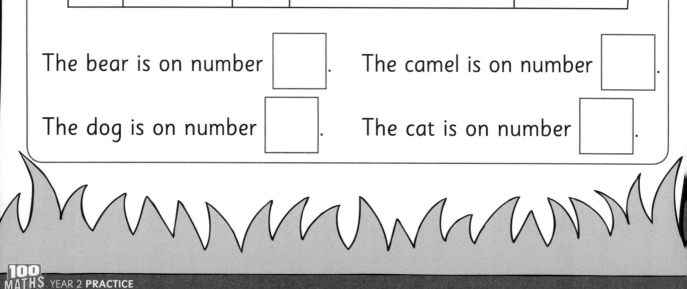

0   10

The bear is on number ☐ .   The camel is on number ☐ .

The dog is on number ☐ .   The cat is on number ☐ .

0   50

The bear is on number ☐ .   The camel is on number ☐ .

The dog is on number ☐ .   The cat is on number ☐ .

Great estimate!

To estimate, ask: Is the number between 0 and 10?
10 and 20? 30 and 40? 50 and 100?

Write your estimate and then count in groups to help you.

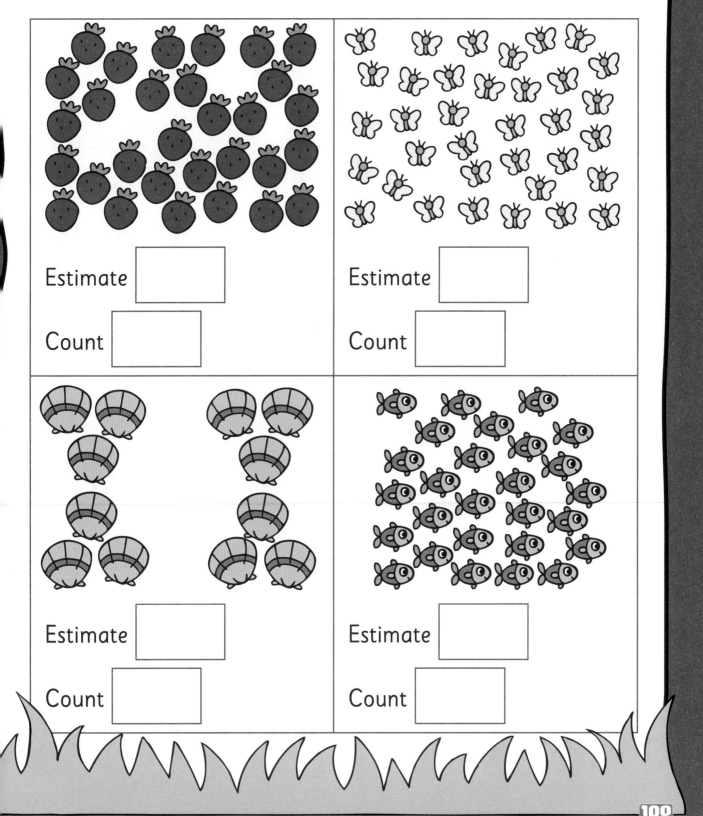

Estimate

Count

Estimate

Count

Estimate

Count

Estimate

Count

Guess the amount

Decide which is the best range for your estimate:
0–10, 10–20, 30–40, 40–50, 50–100?
When counting, it might be easier to mark each pebble as you count it.

1. Guess how many pebbles there are in the jar.

   Write your estimate here.

2. Now count the pebbles.

3. How close was your estimate?

4. What would be a good estimate for three jars of pebbles?

   Explain your estimate.

   _____

   _____

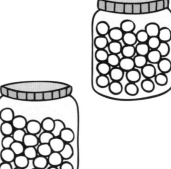

5. Now count all the pebbles in the three jars.

   How close was your estimate?

Writing numbers to 100

Practise writing numbers in numerals and in words.
For **34**, put **thirty** and **four** together to make **thirty-four.**
Try making three-digit numbers.

How many new 2-digit numbers can you find, using the five cards below? Write each number, and its name, in the space below. One has been done for you.

Helpful words	
twenty	two
thirty	three
forty	four
seventy	seven
eighty	eight

| 2 | 3 | 4 | 7 | 8 |

47, forty-seven	

Writing larger numbers

If you can write 2-digit numbers in words, then it is easy to write 3-digit numbers by adding 'one hundred', 'two hundred' and so on.

So, **132** is written as **one hundred and thirty-two**.

Poor Mickey keeps forgetting how to write his numbers. Help him write these numbers.

1. Write 103 in words.

_____

_____

2. Write 'one hundred and eighty-eight' in digits.

3. Write 199 in words.

_____

_____

4. Write 'one hundred
and seventy' in digits.

Place-value problems

For some problems you may have to round your answer up or down.
Sometimes, drawing the items in the problem will help you to solve it. In this problem you could draw boxes and put 10 pencils in each one.

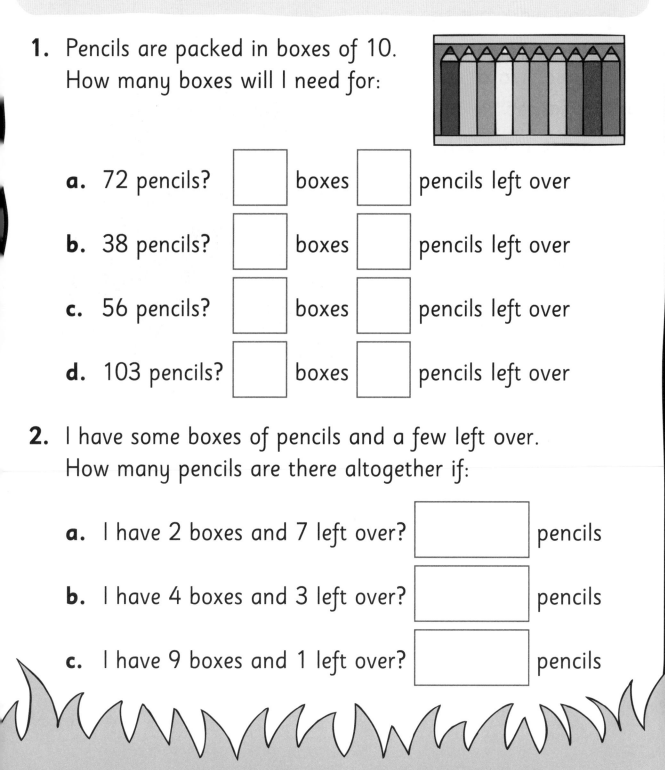

1. Pencils are packed in boxes of 10.
    How many boxes will I need for:

    a. 72 pencils? ☐ boxes ☐ pencils left over

    b. 38 pencils? ☐ boxes ☐ pencils left over

    c. 56 pencils? ☐ boxes ☐ pencils left over

    d. 103 pencils? ☐ boxes ☐ pencils left over

2. I have some boxes of pencils and a few left over.
    How many pencils are there altogether if:

    a. I have 2 boxes and 7 left over? ☐ pencils

    b. I have 4 boxes and 3 left over? ☐ pencils

    c. I have 9 boxes and 1 left over? ☐ pencils

Numbers to 20

Practise adding numbers to 10, as these will help you work out addition to 20.

If you know 1 + 9 = 10, it will help you remember that **11 + 9** = 20.

The 1s are the same. Use cubes to help you work out the bonds to 20.

You have two darts to throw at the target.

You must score 20.

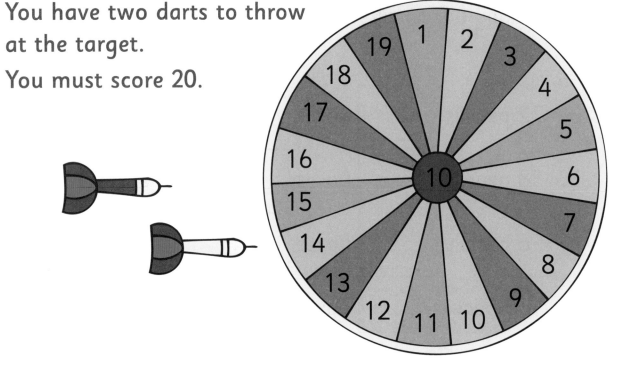

Write the different ways to make 20 using pairs of these numbers.

_____

_____

_____

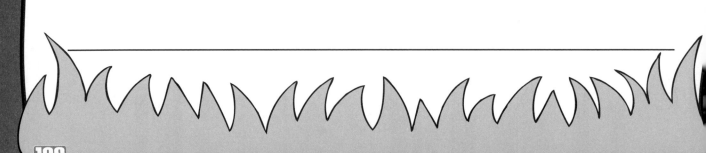

Make 20!

Joe has 20 marbles. He puts some in each of his two pockets.

How many different ways can he do this?

Use the table below to record your work.

Pocket 1	Pocket 2

Numbers to 100

Practise adding numbers to 10.
This will help you add to 100.
Use blocks or cubes to help you
You know that 2 + 8 = 10, so:
20 + 80 = 100.

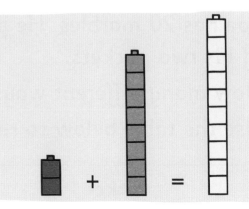

You have two darts to throw at the target.
You must score 100.

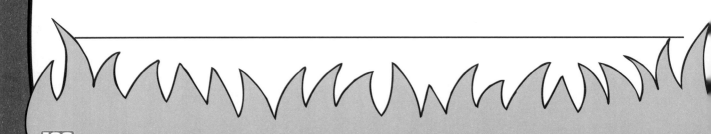

Write the different ways to make 100 using pairs of these numbers.

_____

_____

_____

Perfect Peter has found seven ways to make 100 using any two numbers. He has challenged you to find more.

- Here is one to start you off:
  60 + 40 = 100.

- And here is another one:
  1 + 99 = 100.

1. How many more can you find?

_____

_____

_____

_____

_____

_____

2. Do you think you found them all?

Addition facts

Look at each addition and ask:
Is this a double? Is it a number bond to 20?
Do I need to put the larger number in my head and count on?

1. Find the missing amounts.

a. 5kg + 5kg = ☐ kg

b. 3p + 3p = ☐ p

c. 8cm + 8cm = ☐ cm

d. 3p + ☐ p = 7p

e. ☐ cm + 3cm = 9cm

f. 2kg + ☐ kg = 6kg

2. Write in how many you need to add to each number to make 20.
Like this: ten ☐ 10

a. nine ☐

b. five ☐

c. two ☐

d. eleven ☐

e. thirteen ☐

f. nineteen ☐

3. Answer the questions below using the number line.

0 1 2 3 4 5 6 7 8 9 10 11 12 13 14 15

a. How many steps is it from 5 to 12? ☐

b. How many steps is it from 4 to 15? ☐

Subtraction facts

Subtract means the same as **count back** or **take away.**
If you are subtracting a 1-digit number, put the larger number in your head and count back the smaller number on your fingers. You can also use a number line.

1. Fill in the missing numbers and signs in these sets.

a.	9	–		=	9	→	9	–	9		0
b.		–	1	=	8	→	9	–		=	1
c.	9	–	2	=		→	9		7	=	2
d.	9	–	3		6	→		–	6	=	3
e.	9		4	=	5	→	9	–	5	=	

2. Fill in the blanks. You must use 1- and 2-digit numbers.

a. ☐ – ☐ = 6   b. ☐ – ☐ = 4

c. ☐ – ☐ = 9   d. ☐ – ☐ = 5

e. ☐ – ☐ = 8   f. ☐ – ☐ = 7

3. Answer these questions.

a. What is 14 take away 7? ☐

b. What is six fewer than sixteen? ☐

Addition and subtraction

Knowing an addition fact can help you work out a subtraction fact with the same numbers.
If you know that $5 + 4 = 9$, you can use it to work out that $9 - 5 = 4$.

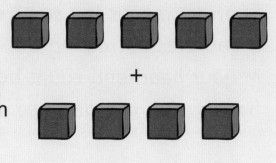

1. Fill in the missing amounts in these two sets.

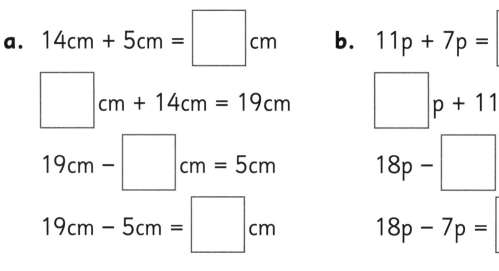

a. $14cm + 5cm = \boxed{} cm$

$\boxed{} cm + 14cm = 19cm$

$19cm - \boxed{} cm = 5cm$

$19cm - 5cm = \boxed{} cm$

b. $11p + 7p = \boxed{} p$

$\boxed{} p + 11p = 18p$

$18p - \boxed{} p = 7p$

$18p - 7p = \boxed{} p$

2. Now answer these questions:

a. $17m + 12m = \boxed{} m$

$\boxed{} m + 17m = 29m$

$29m - \boxed{} m = 17m$

$29m - 17m = \boxed{} m$

b. $30g + 50g = \boxed{} g$

$\boxed{} g + 30g = 80g$

$80g - \boxed{} g = 50g$

$80g - 50g = \boxed{} g$

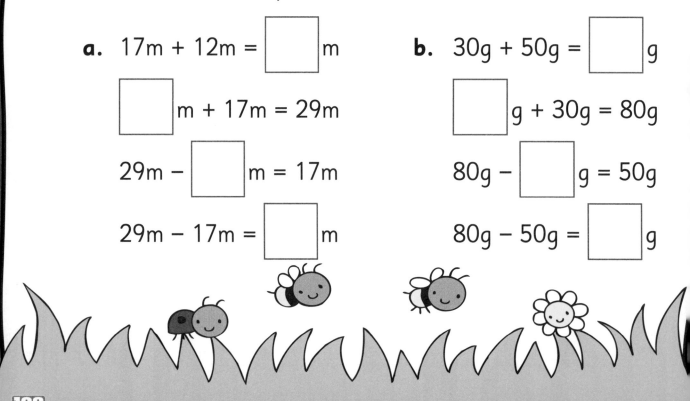

Inverse match

Inverse means the **opposite**. Subtraction is the **inverse** (the opposite) of addition.

Look at the addition $4 + 3 = 7$. The **inverse** is $7 - 3 = 4$.

Tip: The subtraction always starts with the total from the addition.

Draw a line to match each addition to its inverse subtraction.

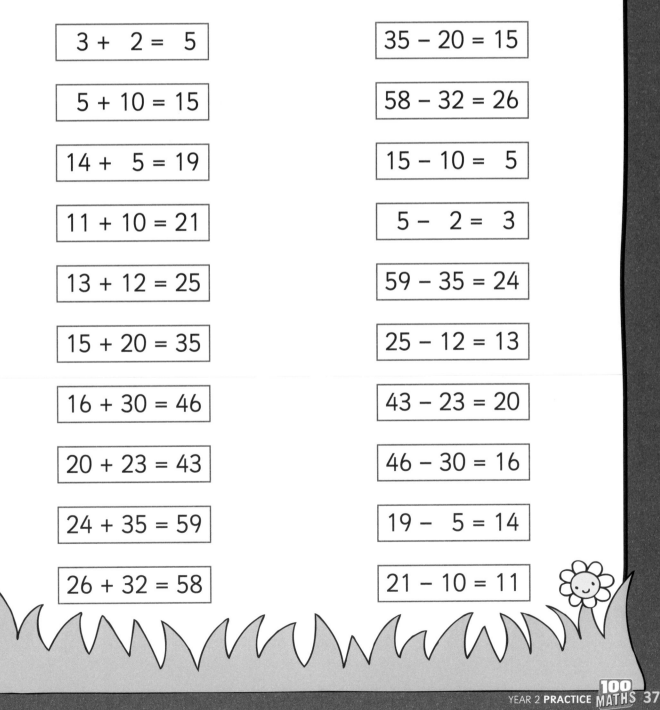

$3 + 2 = 5$	$35 - 20 = 15$
$5 + 10 = 15$	$58 - 32 = 26$
$14 + 5 = 19$	$15 - 10 = 5$
$11 + 10 = 21$	$5 - 2 = 3$
$13 + 12 = 25$	$59 - 35 = 24$
$15 + 20 = 35$	$25 - 12 = 13$
$16 + 30 = 46$	$43 - 23 = 20$
$20 + 23 = 43$	$46 - 30 = 16$
$24 + 35 = 59$	$19 - 5 = 14$
$26 + 32 = 58$	$21 - 10 = 11$

Arrow sentences

Choose two numbers from the boxes and make an arrow sentence.

One example has been done for you, using the numbers 12 and 6.

2	3	4	5	6	7	8	9	10
11	12	13	14	15	16	17		

Missing numbers

Finding missing numbers can be tricky. You can use cubes or a pencil and paper to 'work out' the problem.
Remember to use the inverse operation.

☐ − 17 = 8, then 17 + 8 = 25.

You will then find the missing number (25). 25 − 17 = 8.

Magic Mark has made some of the numbers disappear.
Put the correct numbers back in to the number sentences.

a. 26 − 12 =

b. 31 − ⬭ = 13

c. ⬭ − 23 = 14

d. ⬭ − 20 = 24

e. 36 − ⬭ = 24

f. 17 − ⬭ = 13

g. 29 − 17 =

h. ⬭ − 37 = 11

What's the difference?

To find the difference between two numbers, you need to subtract the smaller number from the larger number. The difference between 19 and 26 is the same as 26 – 19 = 7.

What is the difference between:

1. 12 and 18

2. 21 and 7

3. 23 and 32

4. 16 and 44

5. 29 and 38

6. 31 and 50

7. 47 and 9

8. 15 and 33

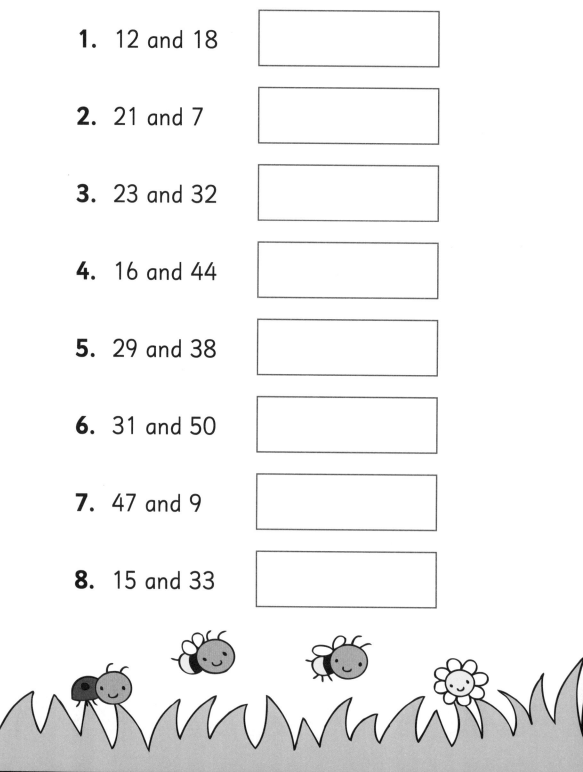

Split the number

When adding try keeping the largest number whole, then split the other number into 10s and 1s before adding them together.

$$23 + \mathbf{12} = 23 + \mathbf{10 + 2} = 33 + 2 = 35.$$

Choose two numbers to add together using partitioning. The first one has been done for you.

| 11 | 15 | 23 | 34 | 41 | 52 |

Numbers:	Partitioning:	Answer:
15 and 23	$23 + 10 + 5 = 33 + 5$	38

Numbers:	Partitioning:	Answer:

Numbers:	Partitioning:	Answer:

Numbers:	Partitioning:	Answer:

Numbers:	Partitioning:	Answer:

Totals and differences

To total 46 + 22, start with 46 (the larger number) and add the 20 (the 10s from 22), then add the 2.

$$46 + 20 = 66 \text{ and } 66 + 2 = 68$$

To find the difference, start with the larger number and split the second number into 10s and 1s.

$$46 - 22: 46 - 20 = 26 \text{ and } 26 - 2 = 24$$

Choose pairs of numbers.

Find the total of the numbers in each pair.

Find the difference of the numbers in each pair.

26   48   59   18   72   34   14

My numbers: ___ and ___ Total _____ Difference _____	My numbers: ___ and ___ Total _____ Difference _____
My numbers: ___ and ___ Total _____ Difference _____	My numbers: ___ and ___ Total _____ Difference _____

Adding order

You can add numbers in any order:
so 5 + 3 = 8, but 3 + 5 = 8 as well.
It is easier to start with the larger number. Put the larger number in your head and count on the smaller number.

1. Rewrite with the larger number first. Then find the totals.

      a. 5 + 13 =   13 + 5   = 18

      b. 8 + 11 = _____ = ____

      c. 3 + 16 = _____ = ____

      d. 6 + 14 = _____ = ____

      e. 5 + 12 = _____ = ____

      f. 3 + 17 = _____ = ____

2. Use each number to make six sums. Put the larger number first each time. Find all the answers.

___ + ___ = ___   (11) (41) (23) (32)   ___ + ___ = ___

___ + ___ = ___   (21) (34) (43) (31)   ___ + ___ = ___

___ + ___ = ___   (44) (13) (42) (22)   ___ + ___ = ___

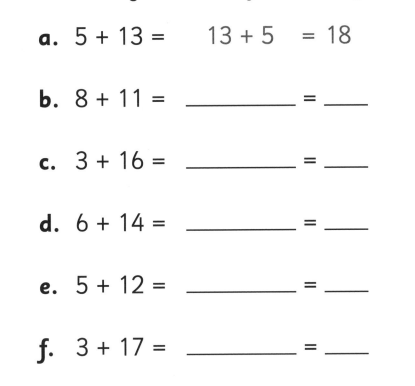
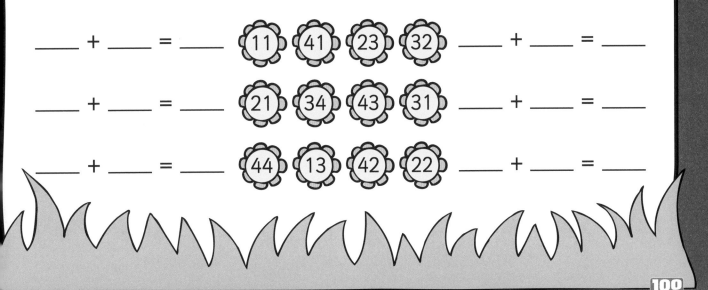

Totals to 10

Adding three numbers is easier if you can find two numbers that total 10, for example, to add 8, 6, and 4: start by adding 6 and 4 (10) and then add 8. 10 + 8 = 18.

Choose three numbers to add together.

Make sure that two of them total 10. Next, add the third number.

| 2   3   4   6   7   8   12   13   14   16   17   18 |

Numbers chosen	Numbers totalling 10	Addition

Adding and subtracting several numbers

You can add numbers in any order, but it is easier to start with the largest number and add smaller numbers to it.
To add 3, 6 and 15, reorder to 15 + 6 + 3.
You **cannot** subtract in any order. You must start with the largest number and subtract the smaller numbers: 15 − 6 − 3.

1. Add these amounts, largest number first.

   a. 1p, 12p, 3p   [   ] p

   b. 2kg, 14kg, 4kg   [   ] kg

   c. 11m, 3m, 5m   [   ] m

   d. 10cm, 3cm, 5cm   [   ] cm

2. Subtract from the largest number.

   a. 12, 3, 2   [   ]

   b. 20, 5, 6   [   ]

   c. 6, 4, 15   [   ]

   d. 3, 25, 7   [   ]

Adding 10s to 2-digit numbers

Practise counting on in 10s from any 2-digit number:
16, 26, 36, 46... the 1s digit always stays the same.
Use your fingers, one finger for each 10. To add 30 to 43,
put 43 in your head and count on three fingers in 10s:
43, 53, 63, 73.

1. The price of these toys has gone up by 20p. Work out the new price.

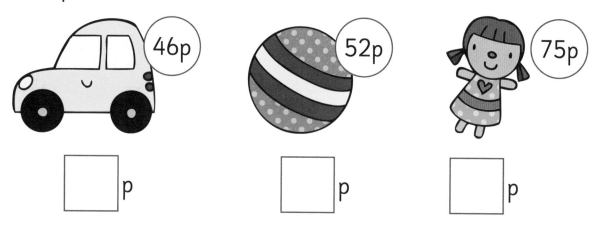

46p ☐p   52p ☐p   75p ☐p

2. These toys now cost 30p more. Work out the new price.

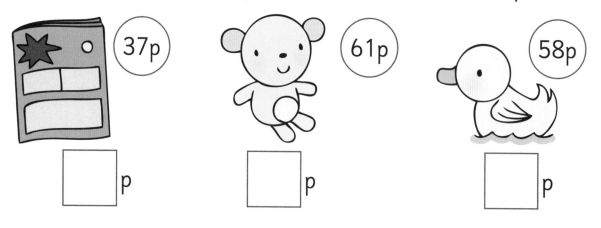

37p ☐p   61p ☐p   58p ☐p

3. Choose one of the toys. It is now 40p more. How much does it cost now?   ☐p

Subtracting 10s from 2-digit numbers

Practise counting back in 10s from any 2-digit number:
68, 58, 48, 38... the 1s digit always stays the same.
To subtract 40 from 73, put 73 in your head and count back
four fingers (one for each 10): 63, 53, 43, 33.

S A L E !

1. The price of these toys has gone down by 30p. Work out
the new price.

46p   52p   75p

☐ p   ☐ p   ☐ p

2. These toys now cost 50p less. Work out the new price.

87p   61p   98p

☐ p   ☐ p   ☐ p

3. Choose one of the toys. It is now 40p less.   ☐ p
How much does it cost now?

Addition problems

Read the problem. Try different methods to solve them.
Write down each correct addition sentence.

1. Unlucky Ducky is trying to make
   the number 13 with these cards.
   How many different ways could
   she do it, using number 6 as one
   of the cards each time?

   _____

   _____

   _____

2. How many ways can you score
   12 by rolling three dice?

   _____

   _____

   _____

Party subtraction problems

Read each problem. Write a subtraction sentence for each one. Work out the answer.

Tip: Each sentence starts with the larger number, 20.

On Saturday, Sam had a birthday party.

1. 20 friends came to his party. 3 were girls. How many were boys?

2. He blew up 20 balloons. 12 were blue. The rest were yellow. How many balloons were yellow?

3. He received 20 presents. 5 were in bags. The rest were in boxes. How many presents were in boxes?

4. He made 20 hats. 14 were stripy. The rest were spotty. How many were spotty?

5. He made 20 sandwiches. 11 were jam. The rest were cheese. How many were cheese?

6. He had 20 candles on his cake. 7 were pink. The rest were orange. How many were orange?

Addition and subtraction

How many more?

Read each problem. Write a subtraction sentence for each one and then work out the answer. The first one has been done for you.

1. How many more than 8 is 14?

$$14 - 8 = 6$$

2. There are 23 black dogs and 12 white dogs. How many more black dogs than white dogs?

$$\boxed{} = \boxed{}$$

3. There are 18 apples and 8 pears. How many more apples than pears?

$$\boxed{} = \boxed{}$$

4. There are 12 rabbits and 15 guinea pigs. How many more guinea pigs than rabbits?

$$\boxed{} = \boxed{}$$

5. There are 50 sweets and 60 chews. How many more chews than sweets?

$$\boxed{} = \boxed{}$$

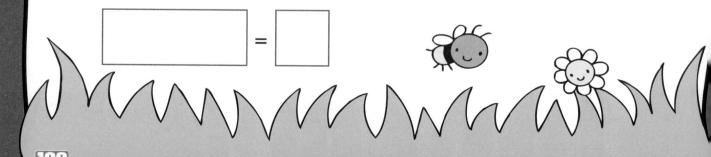

Making money problems

Use real coins and notes to help make and solve these problems. Write a subtraction sentence to help you.

Use these number facts and drawings to make up a problem. Then solve the problem.

£5

£4.50

My problem: _____

The answer: _____

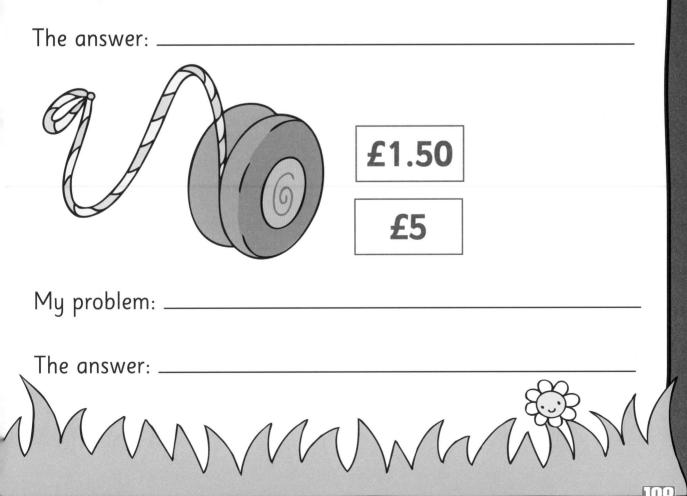

£1.50

£5

My problem: _____

The answer: _____

Addition and subtraction

Money problems

To add pairs of 2-digit numbers, always start with the larger number and add the 10s from the second number. Then add the 1s from the second number.

So, for 35 + 23: 35 + 20 = 55 and 55 + 3 = 58

1. Choose pairs of toys and work out how much they cost.

£13   £18   £25   £21

1st toy costs _____	1st toy costs _____
2nd toy costs _____	2nd toy costs _____
Total cost _____	Total cost _____
How did you work this out?	How did you work this out?
_____	_____
_____	_____

2. How much more is the dolls' house than each of these?

a. the teddy _____   **b.** the digger _____

c. the dinosaur _____

Add to solve the problem

Read each problem and write the addition sentence to solve it. Start with the larger number and add the 10s from the other numbers. Then add the 1s from the other numbers. So for 13 + 12 + 11: 13 + 10 + 10 = 33 and 33 + 2 + 1 = 36

1. Kim and Jim are weighing themselves on a big set of scales. 16 bags of sand balance Kim. 15 bags of sand balance Jim. How many bags of sand are needed to balance both of them together?

2. Charlie the chubby chimp munched 10 bananas plus 11 bananas plus 12 bananas. How many bananas did Charlie munch altogether?

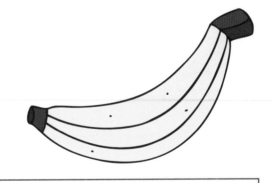

Repeated addition and subtraction

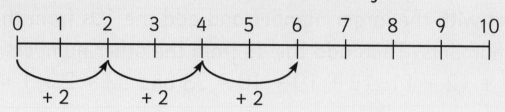

2 × 3 is the same as 2 + 2 + 2, or 3 lots of 2

Complete the number lines by drawing jumps along the lines to show the multiplication in each box.

Write your calculation and the answer underneath each number line.

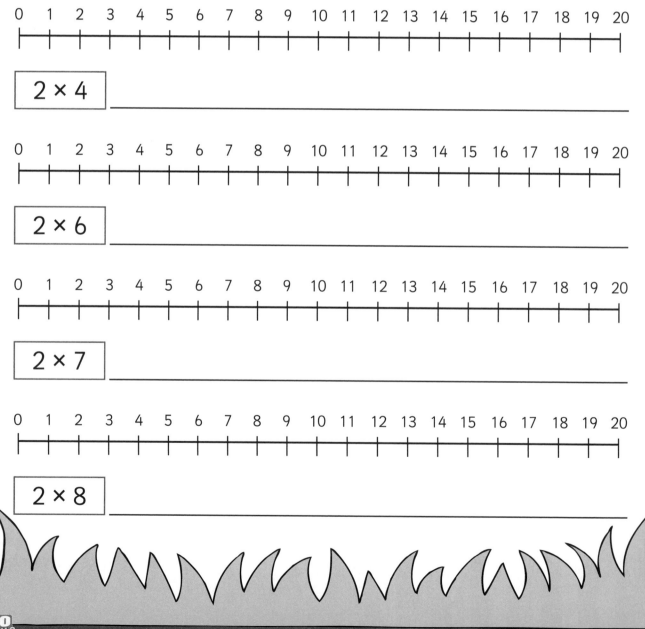

2 × 4

2 × 6

2 × 7

2 × 8

Repeated subtraction can be used to show division.

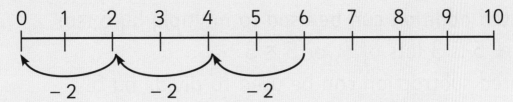

Three lots of 2 have been subtracted so $6 \div 2 = 3$

Complete the number lines by drawing jumps along the lines to show the division in each box.

Write your calculation and the answer underneath each number line.

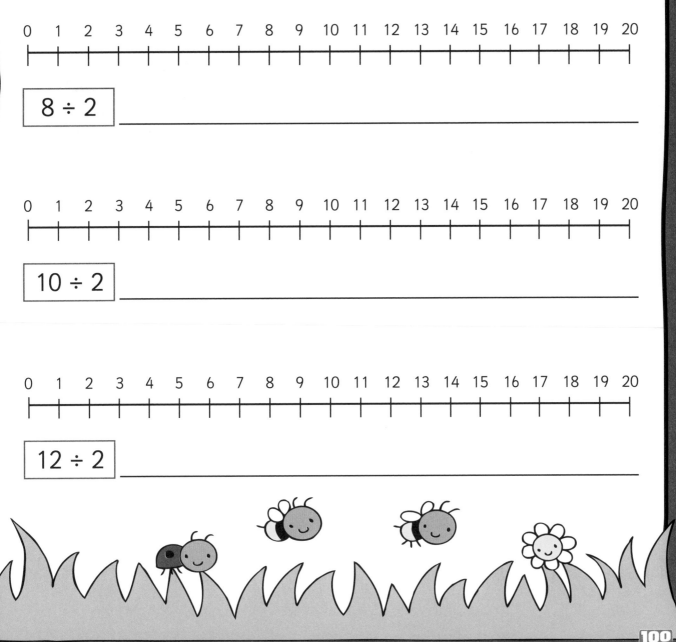

8 ÷ 2 _____

10 ÷ 2 _____

12 ÷ 2 _____

Repeated addition and subtraction (2)

Repeated addition can be used to multiply by 5, so:

5 + 5 + 5 is 3 lots of 5, or 5 × 3

Repeated subtraction can be used to divide by 5.

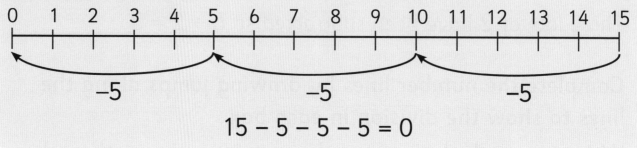

$$15 - 5 - 5 - 5 = 0$$

Complete the number lines by drawing jumps along the lines to show the multiplication or division in each box.

Write your calculation and the answer underneath each number line.

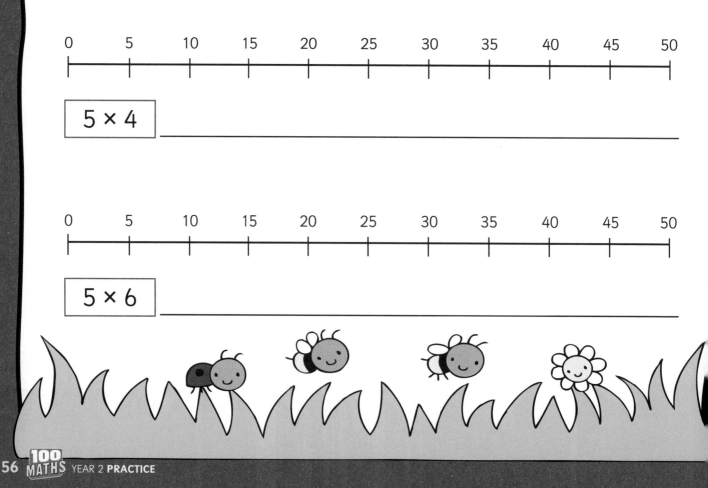

5 × 4 _____

5 × 6 _____

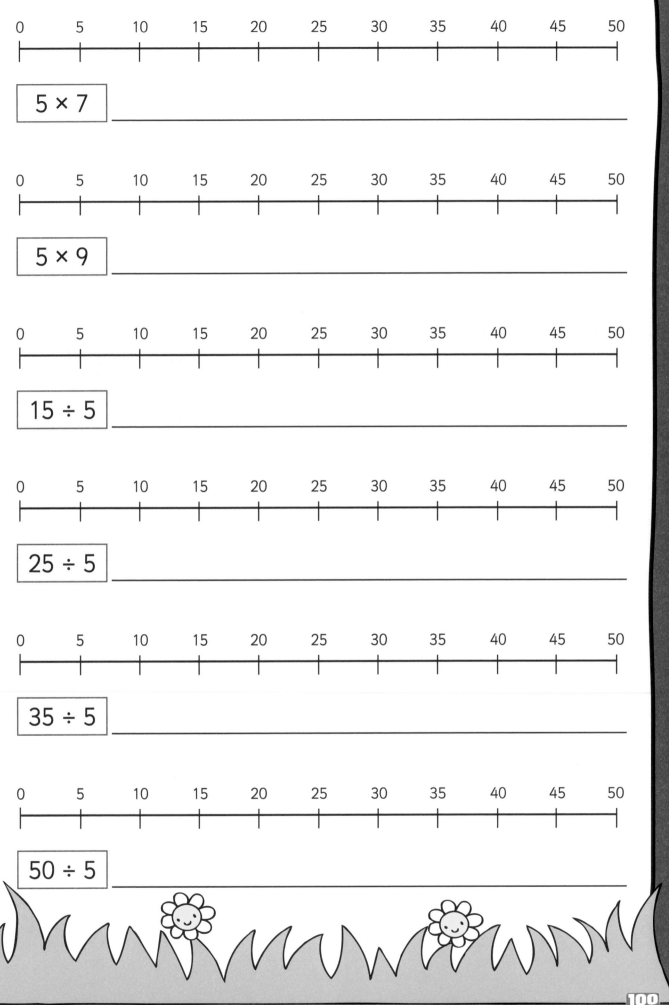

| 0 | 5 | 10 | 15 | 20 | 25 | 30 | 35 | 40 | 45 | 50 |

5 × 7 _____

| 0 | 5 | 10 | 15 | 20 | 25 | 30 | 35 | 40 | 45 | 50 |

5 × 9 _____

| 0 | 5 | 10 | 15 | 20 | 25 | 30 | 35 | 40 | 45 | 50 |

15 ÷ 5 _____

| 0 | 5 | 10 | 15 | 20 | 25 | 30 | 35 | 40 | 45 | 50 |

25 ÷ 5 _____

| 0 | 5 | 10 | 15 | 20 | 25 | 30 | 35 | 40 | 45 | 50 |

35 ÷ 5 _____

| 0 | 5 | 10 | 15 | 20 | 25 | 30 | 35 | 40 | 45 | 50 |

50 ÷ 5 _____

Multiplication and division

Using + and − to multiply and divide by 10

Practise counting on and back in 10s from any 2-digit number and saying the 2-times table. Use repeated addition to multiply by 10, so: 10 + 10 + 10 is the same as 10 × 3. Use repeated subtraction to divide by 10, so: 30 − 10 − 10 − 10 = 0 (3 jumps of 10), or 30 ÷ 10 = 3.

Complete the number lines by drawing jumps along the lines to show the multiplication or division in each box.

Write your calculation and the answer underneath each number line.

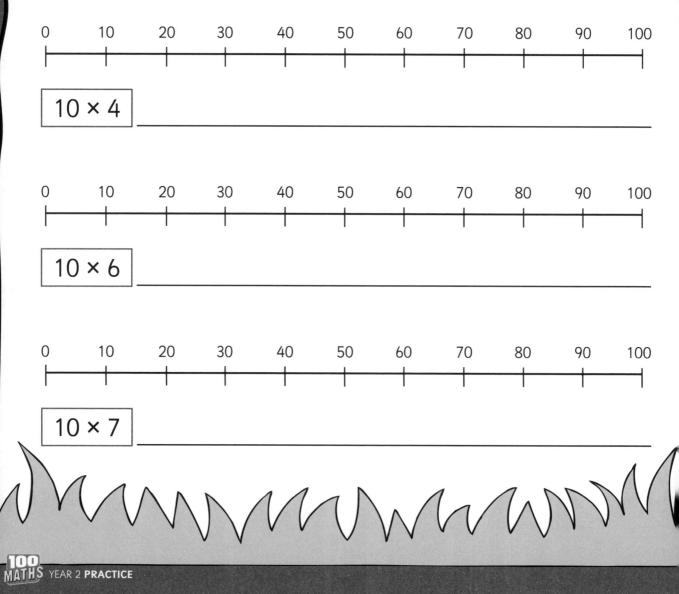

10 × 4

10 × 6

10 × 7

0	10	20	30	40	50	60	70	80	90	100

10 × 9 _____

0	10	20	30	40	50	60	70	80	90	100

30 ÷ 10 _____

0	10	20	30	40	50	60	70	80	90	100

50 ÷ 10 _____

0	10	20	30	40	50	60	70	80	90	100

70 ÷ 10 _____

0	10	20	30	40	50	60	70	80	90	100

100 ÷ 10 _____

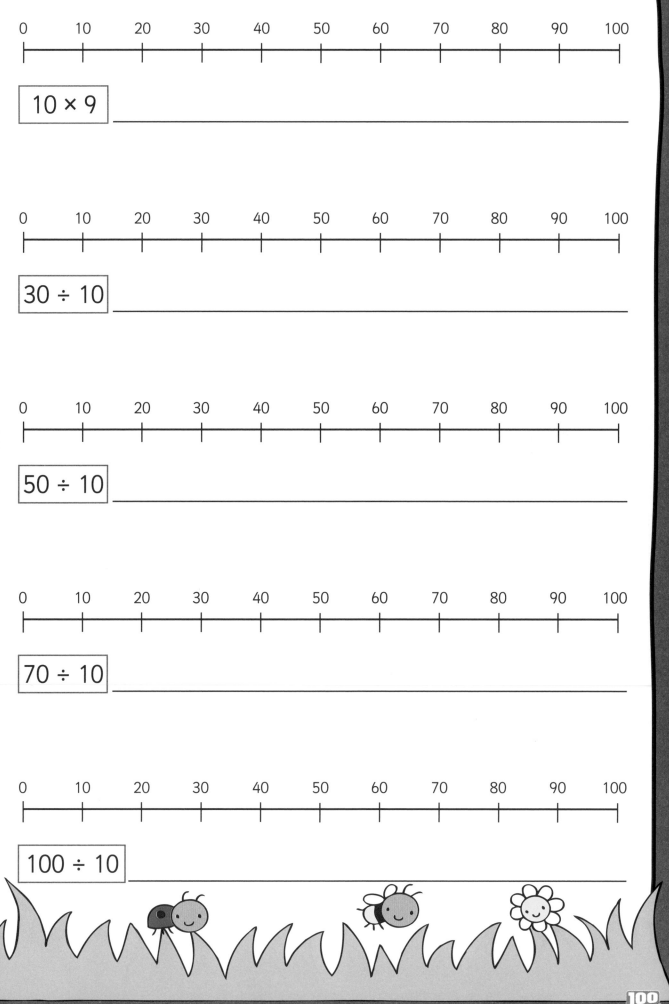

Multiplication arrays

Arrays are arranged in rows and columns and can be used to show us repeated addition and multiplication. This array shows:

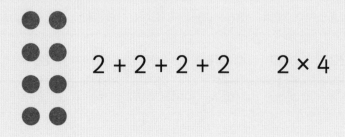

$2 + 2 + 2 + 2$ $2 × 4$

Draw lines to match each array to its repeated addition and multiplication.

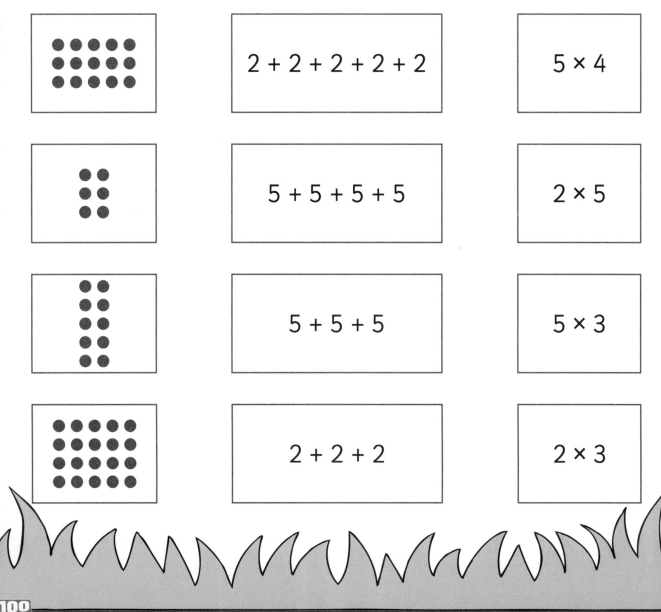

	2 + 2 + 2 + 2 + 2	5 × 4
	5 + 5 + 5 + 5	2 × 5
	5 + 5 + 5	5 × 3
	2 + 2 + 2	2 × 3

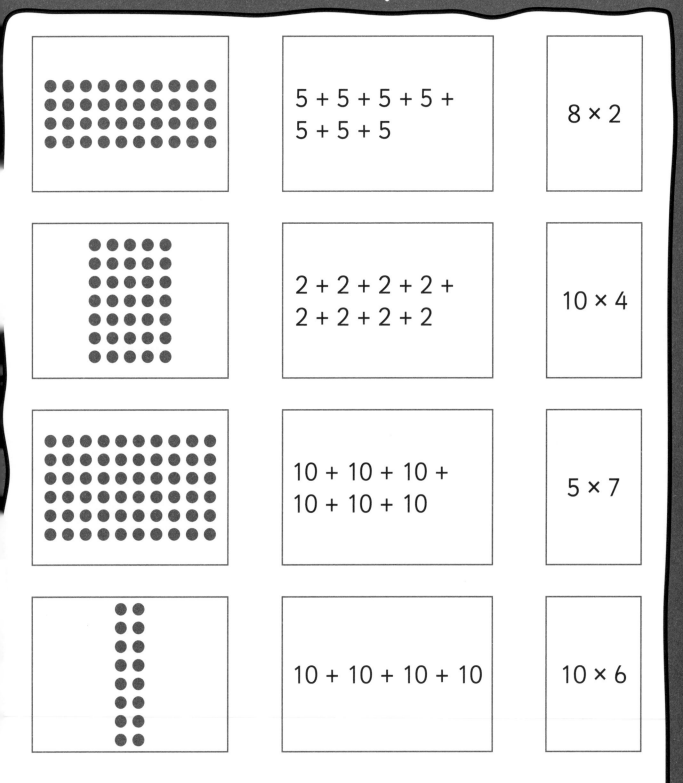

Write the repeated addition and multiplication for:

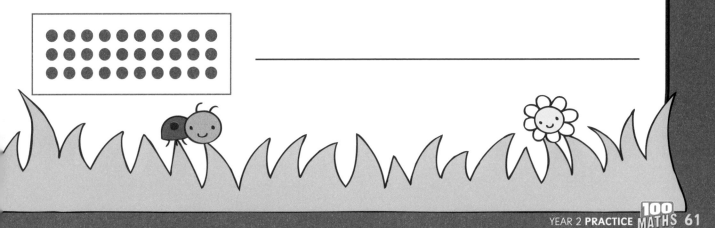

_____

Division arrays

Arrays can also be used to show us division.
You can draw around each group of 2 to find out how many
2s there are in 8, or 8 ÷ 2.

So, this array shows there are 4 groups
of 2 in 8, or 8 ÷ 2 = 4

Match each array to the correct division and work out the
answer. Draw around each group to help you.

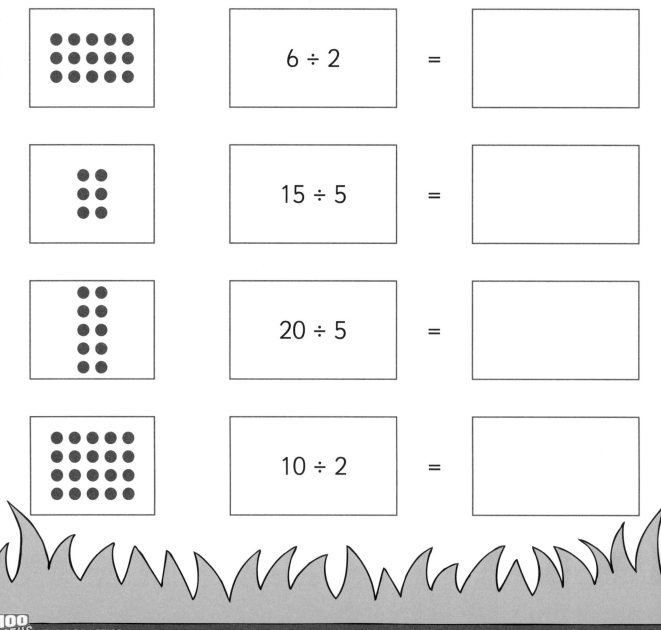

6 ÷ 2   =

15 ÷ 5   =

20 ÷ 5   =

10 ÷ 2   =

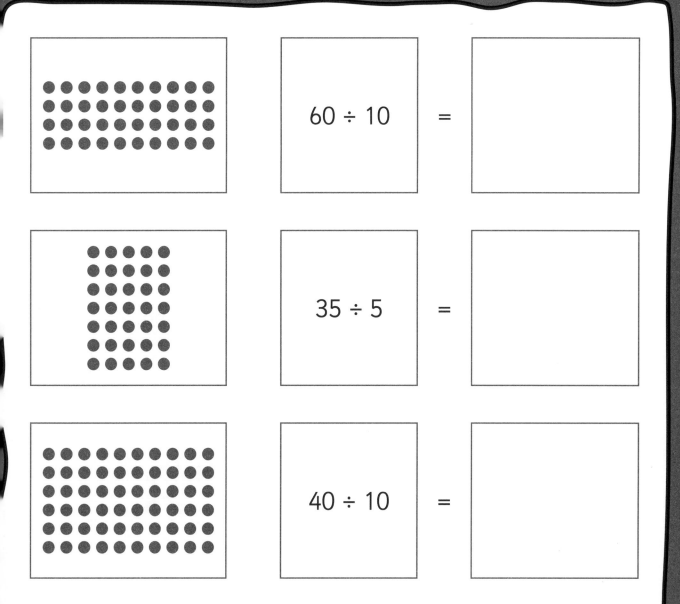

| $60 \div 10$ | = | |

| $35 \div 5$ | = | |

| $40 \div 10$ | = | |

Write the division and answer for:

_____ = _____

Multiples

Multiples of **2** are all the numbers in the 2-times table (2, 4, 6, 8, 10) and always end in those numbers.
Multiples of **5** are the numbers in the 5-times table (5, 10, 15, 20, 25) and always end in 5 or 0.
Multiples of **10** are the numbers in the 10-times table (10, 20, 30, 40, 50) and always end in a 0.

1. Write these numbers under the correct heading.

> 2   10   6   4   25   12   14   16   20
> 5   8   15   18   30   35   25   45   100

Multiples of 2

Multiples of 5

Multiples of 10

2. Circle the numbers below that are multiples of 2, 5 **and** 10.

10   20   25   40   18   36   50

Face the facts

Practise the 2-, 5- and 10-times tables to become quicker at working out number facts in your head.

1. Complete the multiplication grid.

×	2	5	10
2			
4			
1			
5			

2. Complete the multiplication grid.

×	2	5	10
7			
6			
3			
8			

Monster multiplication

Read each problem. Think how many equal groups there are:

  3 + 3 + 3 or 3 × 3.

There are nine eyes altogether.

Write a multiplication number sentence for each group of monsters.

5 monsters with 2 eyes each
2 monsters with 7 eyes each
10 monsters with 3 eyes each
5 monsters with 4 eyes each
6 monsters with 10 eyes each
10 monsters with 5 eyes each
5 monsters with 8 eyes each

Multiplication facts

To work out $\boxed{}$ × 10m = 30m ask: How many 10s are there in 30?

Division will help you: 30 ÷ 10. The missing number is 3. Work out each fact and solve the problem:

1. Fill in the missing amounts.

   a. 2 × 10kg = $\boxed{}$ kg

   b. 6 × $\boxed{}$ p = 12p

   c. $\boxed{}$ × 5cm = 35cm

   d. 4 × $\boxed{}$ m = 40m

   e. 8p × 2 = $\boxed{}$ p

   f. $\boxed{}$ × 5g = 50g

2. Answer these questions.

   a. Nine groups of five. How many altogether? $\boxed{}$

   b. Seven times two equals? $\boxed{}$

3. Complete the grid.

×	0	1	2	3	4	5	6	7	8	9	10
2										18	
10						50					

Division facts

To work out 16p ÷ ☐ = 8p, ask yourself: How many 8s are there in 16?

Multiplication will help you: 2 × 8 = 16

Use counters and put them into equal groups.

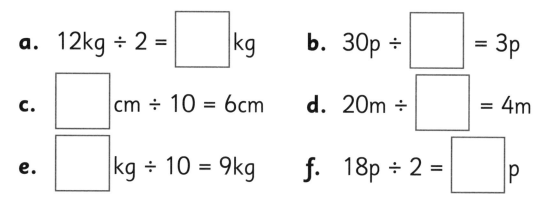

1. Fill in the missing amounts.

   a. 12kg ÷ 2 = ☐ kg

   b. 30p ÷ ☐ = 3p

   c. ☐ cm ÷ 10 = 6cm

   d. 20m ÷ ☐ = 4m

   e. ☐ kg ÷ 10 = 9kg

   f. 18p ÷ 2 = ☐ p

2. Divide into equal groups of two. Write how many groups there are.

   a. 14 tennis balls ☐

   b. 10 fish ☐

3. How many:

   a. Twos in eight? ☐

   b. Tens in forty? ☐

   c. Fives in twenty? ☐

   d. Twos in eighteen? ☐

   e. Fives in fifteen? ☐

   f. Tens in seventy? ☐

Relationship between × and ÷

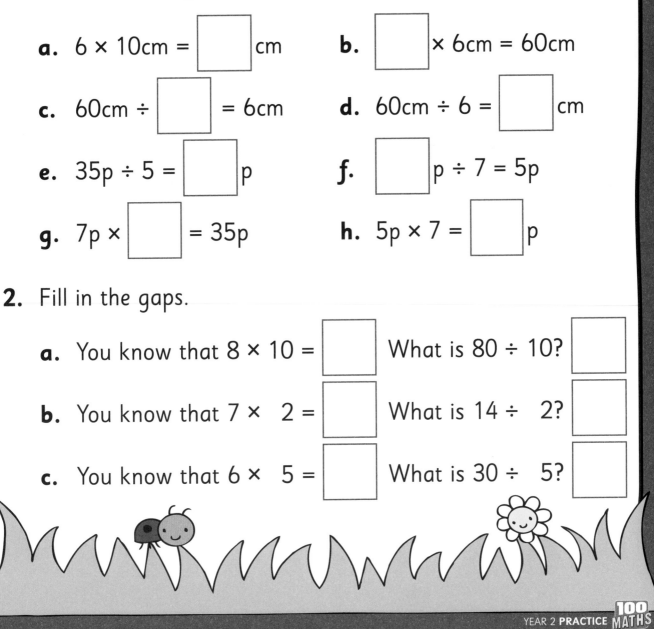

$4 × 10 = 40$ **and** $10 × 4 = 40$

You can multiply in any order and the answer stays the same. But you **cannot** divide numbers in any order: $40 ÷ 10 = 4$ (there are 4 rows), but $10 ÷ 40 = \frac{1}{4}$, not 4.

1. Find the missing numbers.

a. $6 × 10\text{cm} = \boxed{}\text{cm}$

b. $\boxed{} × 6\text{cm} = 60\text{cm}$

c. $60\text{cm} ÷ \boxed{} = 6\text{cm}$

d. $60\text{cm} ÷ 6 = \boxed{}\text{cm}$

e. $35\text{p} ÷ 5 = \boxed{}\text{p}$

f. $\boxed{}\text{p} ÷ 7 = 5\text{p}$

g. $7\text{p} × \boxed{} = 35\text{p}$

h. $5\text{p} × 7 = \boxed{}\text{p}$

2. Fill in the gaps.

a. You know that $8 × 10 = \boxed{}$ What is $80 ÷ 10?$ $\boxed{}$

b. You know that $7 × 2 = \boxed{}$ What is $14 ÷ 2?$ $\boxed{}$

c. You know that $6 × 5 = \boxed{}$ What is $30 ÷ 5?$ $\boxed{}$

Multiplication order

3×2 is the same as $2 \times 3 = 6$.

Knowing one multiplication fact helps us to know another one. You can multiply numbers in **any** order and the answer is the same.

1. Below each multiplication fact, write another which gives the same answer. The first one has been done for you.

   a. $3 \times 2 = 6$ **b.** $2 \times 1 = 2$ **c.** $4 \times 2 = 8$

   $2 \times 3 = 6$ _____   _____

   d. $2 \times 5 = 10$ **e.** $5 \times 3 = 15$ **f.** $5 \times 7 = 35$

   _____   _____   _____

   g. $2 \times 7 = 14$ **h.** $9 \times 5 = 45$ **i.** $2 \times 9 = 18$

   _____   _____   _____

2. Solve the problem.

   Five 2p coins have the same value as _____ coins.

Odd and even multiples

Even numbers always end with 2, 4, 6, 8 or 0 – they are always **multiples of 2**. So 34 is an even number, because it ends in a 4. Numbers that end in 1, 3, 5, 7 or 9 are **odd** numbers.
Some multiples of 5 are odd numbers and some are even.

1. Circle all the even numbers.

> 6   13   38   27   42   59   60   102   24   75

2. Write the missing odd numbers.

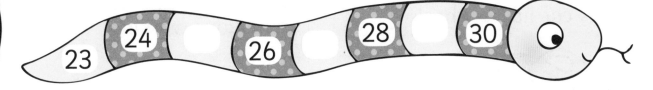

23   24   26   28   30

3. Write these numbers in the correct box. One goes in more than one box.

> 8   15   30   42   25

	Multiples of 2	Multiples of 5
Odd numbers		
Even numbers		

Multiplication and division problems

Read each problem and write a multiplication or division sentence to work out the answer. Draw the answer if necessary. One has been done for you.

1. There are 6 flowers. Put 3 flowers in a vase.

How many vases are needed? 2

Show your working.

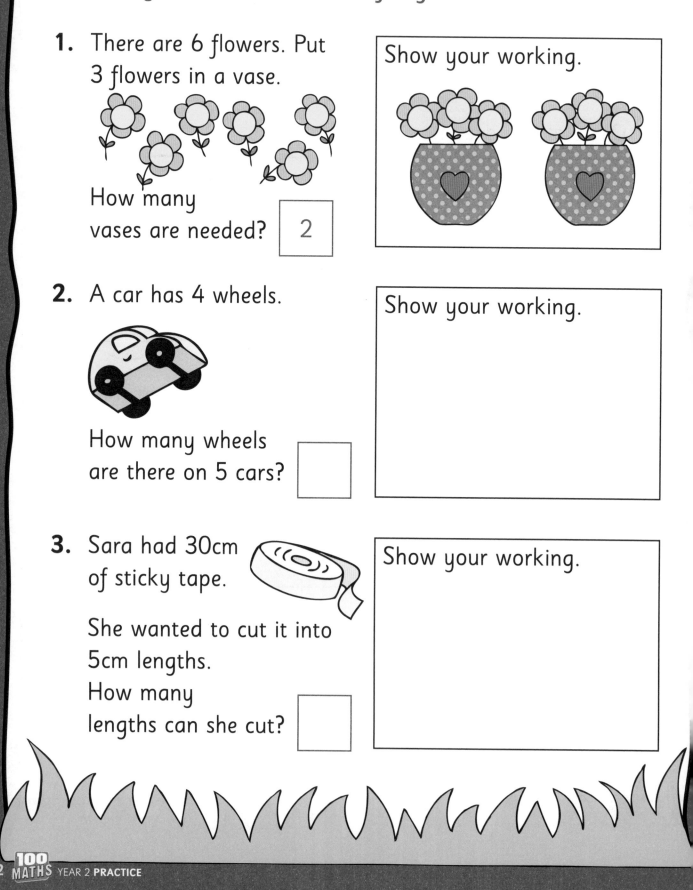

2. A car has 4 wheels.

How many wheels are there on 5 cars?

Show your working.

3. Sara had 30cm of sticky tape.

She wanted to cut it into 5cm lengths.
How many lengths can she cut?

Show your working.

4. Generous Jenna is sharing out her gobstoppers.

She has 30 gobstoppers and shares them equally with five of her friends.

How many gobstoppers does each friend get?

5. There are five floors in this multi-storey car park.

There are seven cars parked on each floor.

How many cars are there in the car park in total?

Fraction wall

A fraction is a part of a whole, for example $\frac{1}{2}$

A fraction wall shows us how many of each fraction
= 1 whole, $\frac{1}{2} + \frac{1}{2}$ = 1 whole $\frac{2}{2}$ also = 1 whole

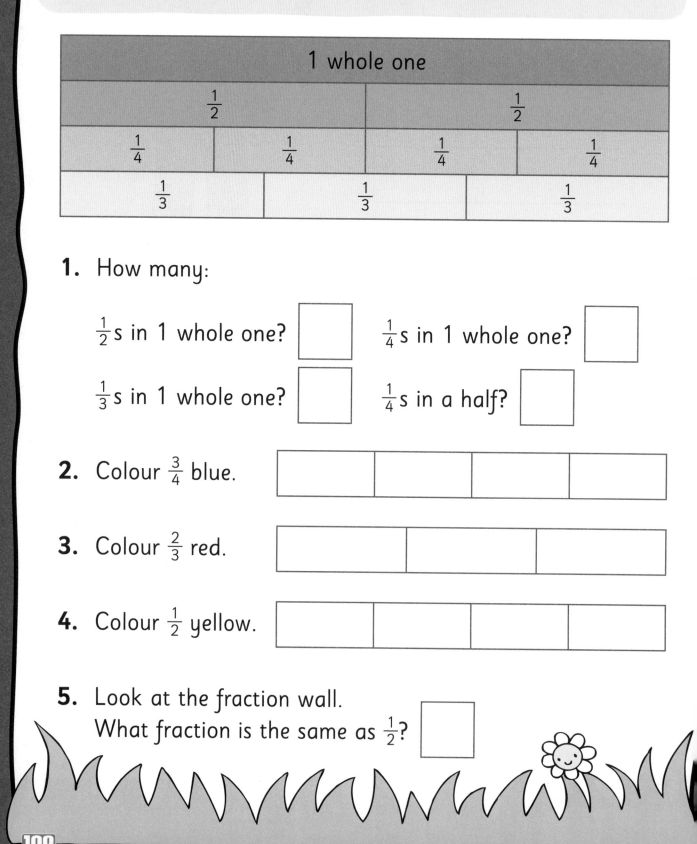

1 whole one			
$\frac{1}{2}$		$\frac{1}{2}$	
$\frac{1}{4}$	$\frac{1}{4}$	$\frac{1}{4}$	$\frac{1}{4}$
$\frac{1}{3}$	$\frac{1}{3}$		$\frac{1}{3}$

1. How many:

$\frac{1}{2}$s in 1 whole one? ☐ $\frac{1}{4}$s in 1 whole one? ☐

$\frac{1}{3}$s in 1 whole one? ☐ $\frac{1}{4}$s in a half? ☐

2. Colour $\frac{3}{4}$ blue.

3. Colour $\frac{2}{3}$ red.

4. Colour $\frac{1}{2}$ yellow.

5. Look at the fraction wall.
What fraction is the same as $\frac{1}{2}$? ☐

Equivalent fractions

Remember: $\frac{4}{4}$ is the same as $\frac{1}{4} + \frac{1}{4} + \frac{1}{4} + \frac{1}{4}$

$\frac{4}{4}$ is the same as 1 whole one

1. For each shape, match the shaded area to the corresponding fraction.

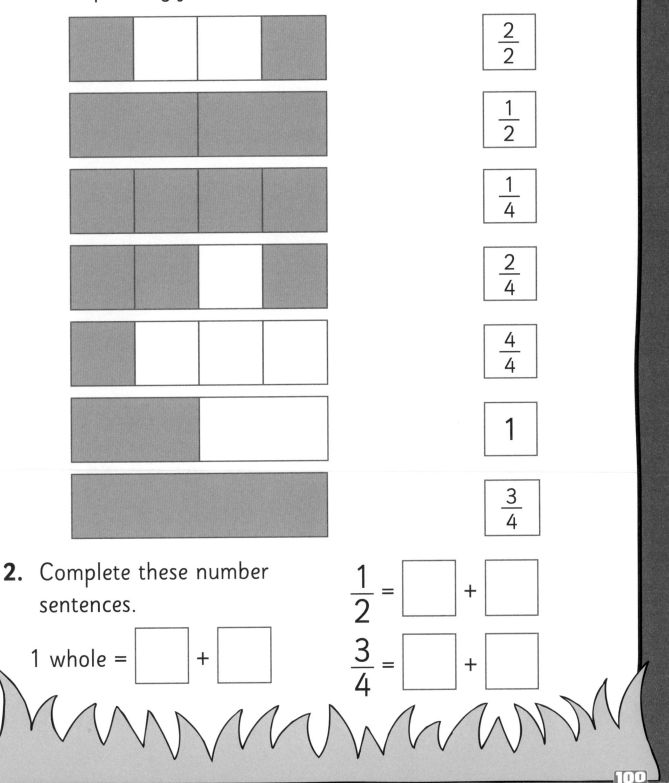

2. Complete these number sentences.

1 whole = ☐ + ☐

$\frac{1}{2}$ = ☐ + ☐

$\frac{3}{4}$ = ☐ + ☐

Fractions

Three-quarters

To find $\frac{3}{4}$ of 8: count out the number of objects (8) and then split into 4 equal groups.
Each group will be $\frac{1}{4}$ of 8
3 groups = $\frac{3}{4}$ (6)

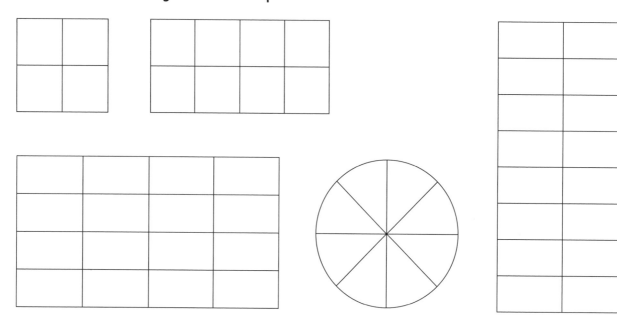

1. Colour $\frac{3}{4}$ of each shape.

2. Draw a circle around $\frac{3}{4}$ of these groups of objects.

Fractions of shapes

Count the number of squares (or parts) in each shape, below. To find $\frac{1}{2}$, split this number into 2 parts. To find $\frac{1}{4}$, split this number into 4 parts.

Colour half of each shape.

Using a different colour, colour a quarter of each shape.

Fractions

Fractions of objects

Amount	$\frac{1}{2}$	$\frac{1}{4}$	$\frac{3}{4}$
8	4	2	6
12	6	3	9
15	No	No	No

Drop a handful of cubes, counters or other small object onto a table. Count how many there are.

Fill in the table to show a half, a quarter and three-quarters of the amount. Repeat 5 times.

Amount	$\frac{1}{2}$	$\frac{1}{4}$	$\frac{3}{4}$

Fractions of measures

1. Rashid has cut each ribbon in half.
Write the new measurement.

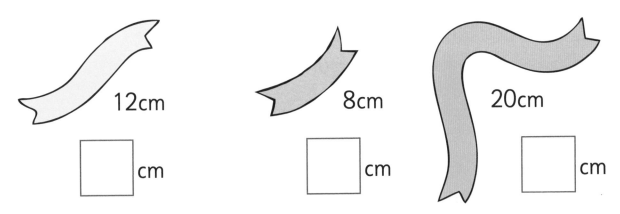

12cm

☐ cm

8cm

☐ cm

20cm

☐ cm

2. Ella has used $\frac{1}{4}$ of the sugar from each scale.
Write the new mass.

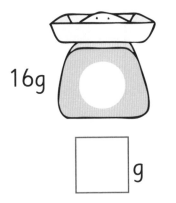 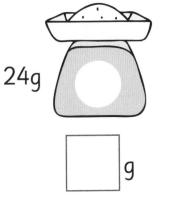 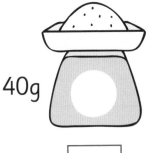

16g

☐ g

24g

☐ g

40g

☐ g

3. Lucas has poured out $\frac{3}{4}$ of the liquid from each jug.
Write the new capacity.

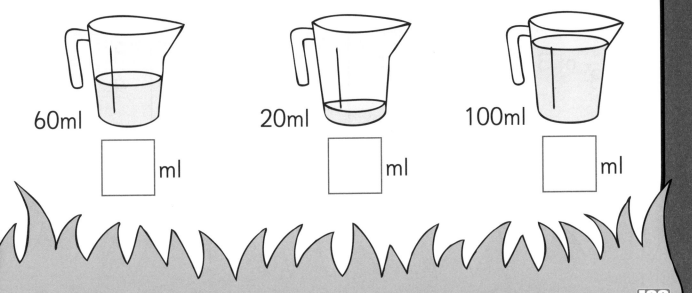

60ml

☐ ml

20ml

☐ ml

100ml

☐ ml

Fractions

Fraction pairs

Look at these examples: What is $\frac{1}{2}$ of 6, $\frac{1}{3}$ of 12 and $\frac{1}{4}$ of 24? These fractions all have 1 as the top number, so to work out the answers simply divide by the bottom number.

$\frac{1}{2}$ of 6 is $6 \div 2 = 3$ $\frac{1}{3}$ of 12 is $12 \div 3 = 4$

$\frac{1}{4}$ of 24 is $24 \div 4 = 6$

Write the answer to each question in the box then draw a line to match the fraction pairs.

$\frac{1}{2}$ of 4

$\frac{1}{4}$ of 20

$\frac{1}{2}$ of 8

$\frac{1}{3}$ of 9

$\frac{1}{4}$ of 12

$\frac{1}{4}$ of 8

$\frac{1}{2}$ of 10

$\frac{1}{4}$ of 16

$\frac{1}{3}$ of 3

$\frac{1}{4}$ of 4

$\frac{2}{4}$ of 24

$\frac{3}{4}$ of 16

Fractions on a number line

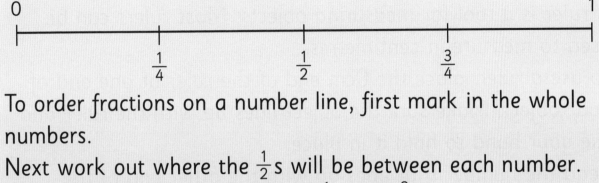

To order fractions on a number line, first mark in the whole numbers.

Next work out where the $\frac{1}{2}$s will be between each number.

This will help you when placing $\frac{1}{4}$s and $\frac{3}{4}$s.

Draw a line to show where the cards appear on the number line.

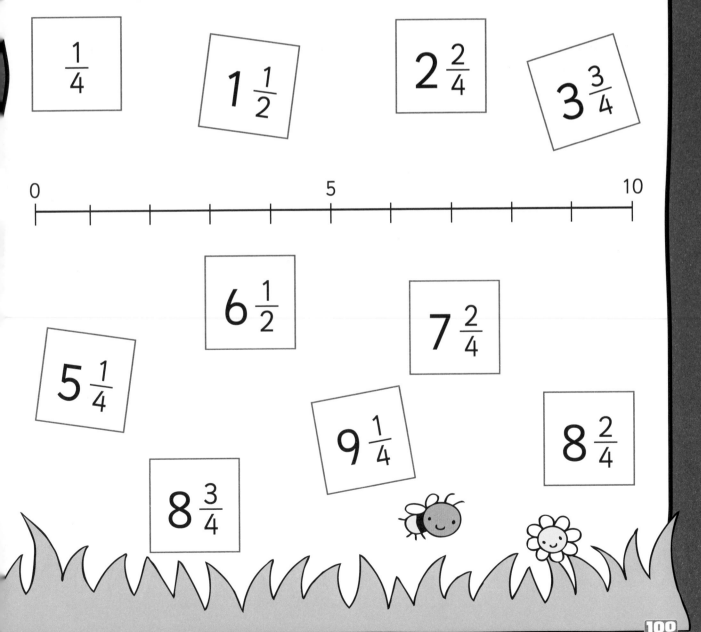

Measurement

Measuring lengths in cm

A ruler is a tool for measuring objects. Most rulers can be used to measure in centimetres.

To use a ruler, place the 0cm end of the ruler at one end of your object. Make sure the object lines up with the ruler and use your hand to hold it in place.

Read the number that lines up with the other end of the object to get your measurement.

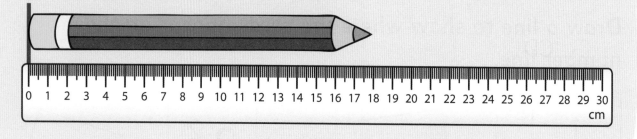

Use a ruler to measure the length of each object in cm.

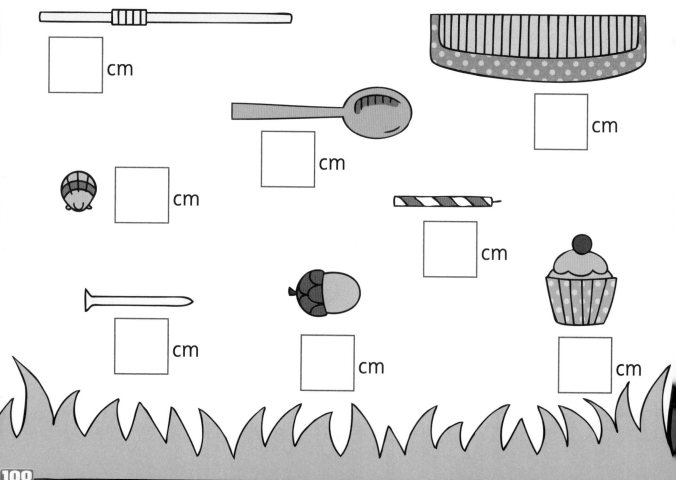

How long is it?

Look at a ruler and then look at objects around you.
Try to estimate the length of a range of objects using the ruler as a guide.
An 'estimate' is a good guess.

You will need: a ruler, a number of household objects.

Object	Estimate (cm)	Actual length (cm)
CD		
Telephone		
Newspaper		
Teaspoon		
Favourite toy		

1. Find the objects listed around the house.

2. Estimate their lengths in centimetres (cm) and write your estimate in the table.

3. Measure the objects with your ruler and write the actual lengths in the table.

4. How close were your estimates to the final measurement?

Weighing in kg and g

A litre bottle filled with water has about the same mass as 1 kilogram.

A paper clip has about the same mass as 1 gram.

Use this knowledge to help you estimate the mass of heavier or lighter objects.

Tip: There are 1000g in 1kg.

Choose five things to weigh.

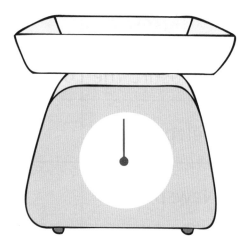

1. Estimate first.

2. Write your estimate.

3. Use kitchen scales to weigh your item in kg and g.

4. Write your measurement.

I am going to weigh	Estimate	Mass

Measuring capacity using l and ml

A milk bottle has a capacity of 1 litre and a teaspoon has a capacity of about 5ml.
Use this knowledge to help you estimate the capacity of larger and smaller containers.
Tip: There are 1000ml in 1 litre.

Choose six different-sized containers to measure.

1. Write your estimate for each container.

2. Measure the container and write the capacity in l and ml.
   Use a measuring jug and a 5ml teaspoon.

Container	My estimate	My measure

Measuring temperature

We use a thermometer to measure temperature. Temperature is usually measured in degrees Celsius (°C).

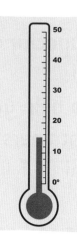

The temperature is 15°C

1. Write the correct temperature for each thermometer.

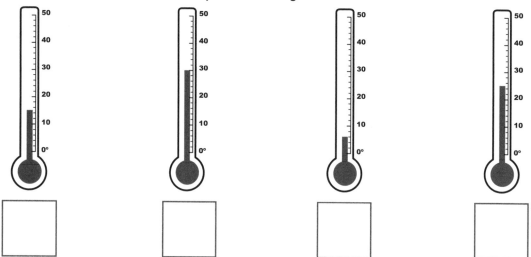

2. Mark each thermometer to show the correct temperature.

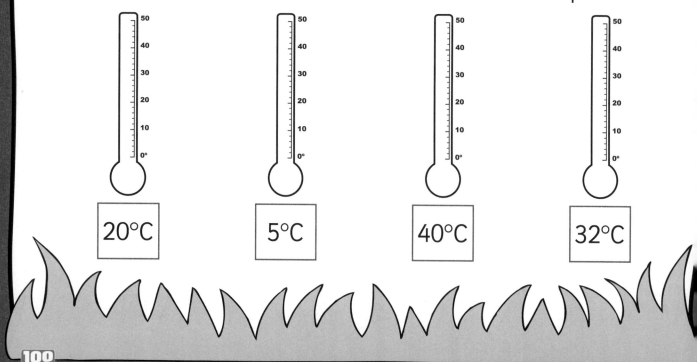

20°C   5°C   40°C   32°C

Reading scales

All of these scales are types of number line, some are in straight lines and some are curved lines.

Read the scales to work out the answers.

Count along each scale and try to give an accurate reading.

The bananas weigh

_____ kg.

The oranges weigh

just over _____ kg.

The ribbon is _____ cm.

There are _____ litres of liquid.

There are _____ litres of liquid.

Measurement

Draw the measures

Work out the measurements on each scale.
Tip: 3.5 is the same as $3\frac{1}{2}$, so would be halfway between 3 and 4.

1. Draw an arrow to show 15cm.

2. Draw an arrow to show a measurement between 15cm and 20cm.

3. Draw an arrow to show half a litre.

4. Draw an arrow to show quarter of a litre.

5. Draw an arrow to show 4.5kg.

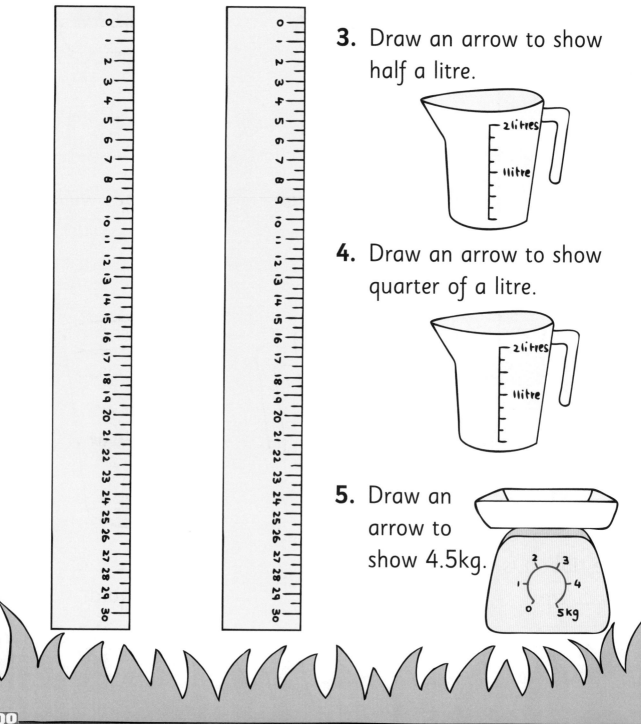

Nature trail problems

Otter Class have been on a nature trail.
They measured a number of things using different measuring instruments.

Read the scales and write the correct measurement under each one.

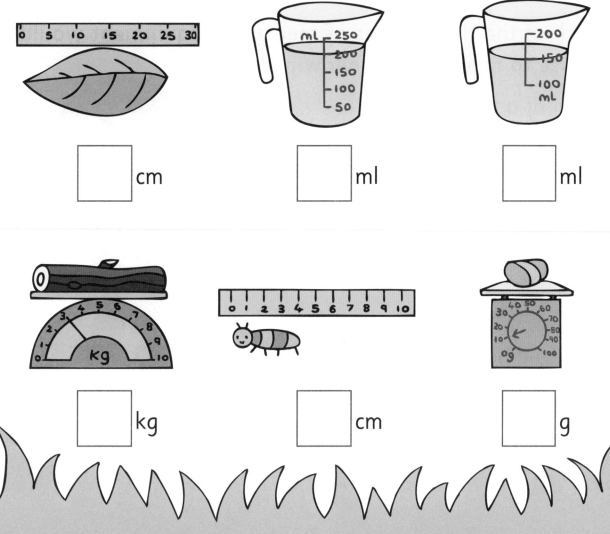

☐ cm

☐ ml

☐ ml

☐ kg

☐ cm

☐ g

Measuring equipment

Tips for measuring:

- A **tape measure** bends and is good for measuring round things.

- A **metre rule** does not bend and is good for measuring straight objects.

- A **trundle wheel** measures larger distances.

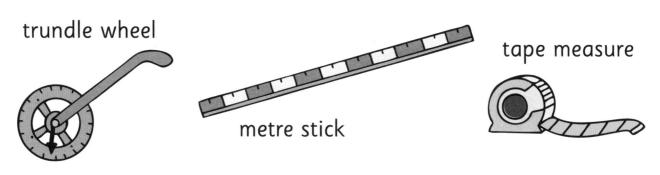

trundle wheel

metre stick

tape measure

Which of the three pieces of measuring equipment would you use to measure the following?

Length of a football pitch

_____

Height of a goalpost

_____

Distance around a football

_____

Distance round my head

_____

Height of a tree

_____

Width of kitchen

_____

Length of garden

_____

Height of car

_____

Width of door

_____

Distance round your chest

_____

Comparing measures

When you order objects, ask yourself: Which is the heaviest/ lightest? Which is the next heaviest? You can use real objects to compare more accurately.

1. Order these objects from lightest to heaviest.

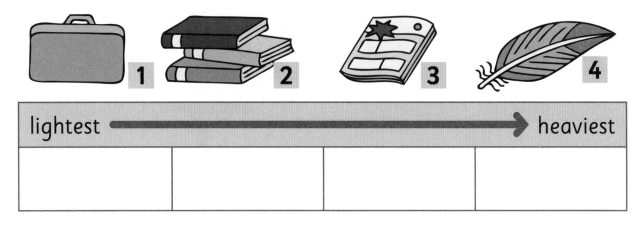

lightest →			heaviest

2. Find an object which = the mass of a banana.

_____

3. Order these objects from shortest to longest.

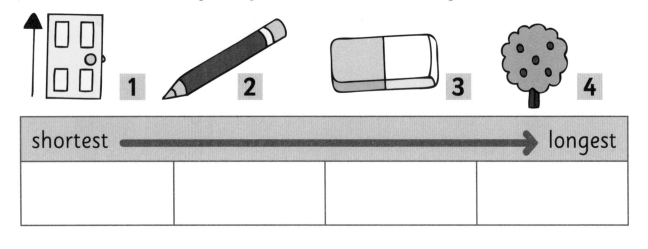

shortest →			longest

4. Find an object with a length < a pencil: _____

5. Order these objects from smallest capacity to biggest capacity.

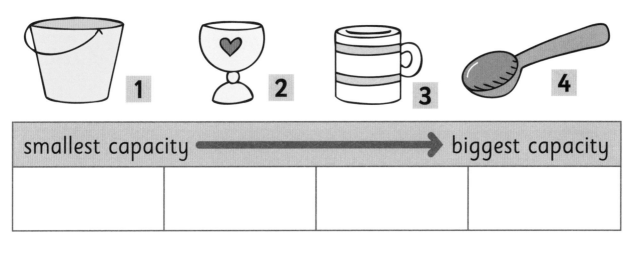

smallest capacity ——————————————➤ biggest capacity			

6. Find an object with a capacity which is > a mug.

_____

7. Order these objects from coldest to hottest.

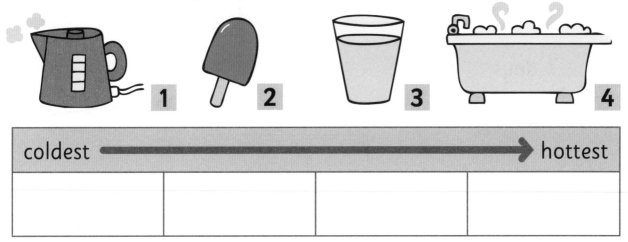

coldest ——————————————————➤ hottest			

8. Find something with a temperature < a kettle but > than a glass of juice.

_____

Time intervals

Think about different units of time.
Practice working out how many seconds there are in a minute, days in a week or weeks in a year.
Use a calendar to help you.

Draw a line to match each pair.

| 1 fortnight | | 1 minute |

60 seconds

| 60 minutes | | 24 hours |

1 hour

| 7 days | | 1 year |

1 day

2 weeks

1 week

52 weeks

| 120 seconds | | 2 minutes |

Telling the time

Practise telling the time to the hour, then to half-hour and quarter-hour intervals.

Learn to match with 3:00

Remember: The big hand measures the minutes.
The little hand measures the hours.

Draw lines to connect the matching clock faces to the correct times.

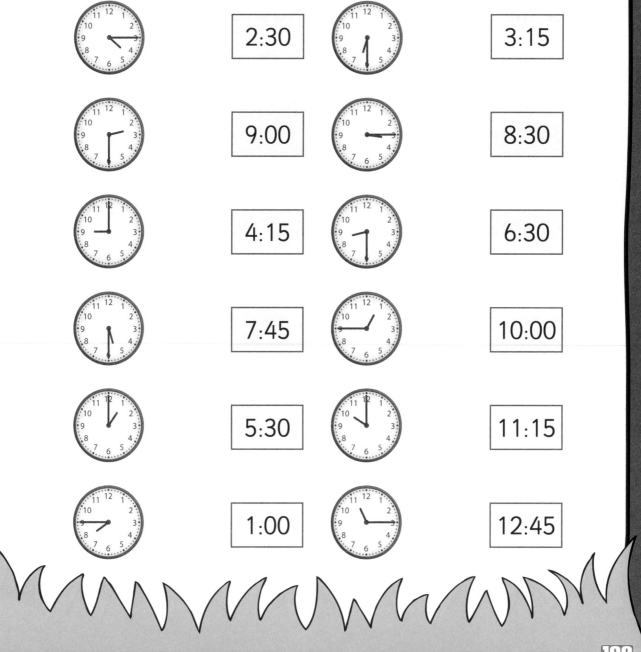

2:30

3:15

9:00

8:30

4:15

6:30

7:45

10:00

5:30

11:15

1:00

12:45

Time problems

Practise counting round a clock from 0 in 5-minute intervals to 60. Practise telling the time to 5-minute intervals.

Tip: 2:15 = quarter past two;
2:30 = half past two;
2:45 = quarter to three.
To work out 40 minutes after 2:05, start at five-minutes past and count on 40 minutes, to 2:45.

The time is five past two or 2:05.

Draw the time on each clock to answer these problems.

1. Sam starts walking to school at 8:25. It takes him 30 minutes. What time does he arrive?

2. Emma starts reading her book at half past six and finishes it 45 minutes later. What time does she finish it?

3. A football game starts at quarter past three and finishes 1 hour and 30 minutes later. What time does the game finish?

4. Katy puts a cake in the oven at 3:10. It needs 35 minutes cooking time. What time does she need to take it out?

Use the timetable to help you answer the questions.

Programme	Start	End
Monster Magic	4:25	4:50
Undersea Adventures	5:10	5:55
Robot Story	6:35	7:45
Policeman Paul	3:05	3:25

5. How long is:

a. Monster Magic? _____

b. Undersea Adventures? _____

c. Robot Story? _____

d. Policeman Paul? _____

6. What is the longest programme?

_____

7. If I watch the two longest programmes, how long will I spend watching television?

_____

Pence to pounds

Tip: 100p = £1.00. The pounds and the pence are separated by a full stop.

So 375p = £3.75

£s   pence

To add amounts of money, work out the answer mentally and then use real coins to check your answer.

Look at the numbers below. For each example, change the number of pence into pounds and pence.

125p ⟶ £1.25   302p ⟶ _____

175p ⟶ _____   345p ⟶ _____

225p ⟶ _____   269p ⟶ _____

180p ⟶ _____   199p ⟶ _____

Write the answers in pounds and pence.

50p + 80p   _____   60p + 90p   _____

70p + 80p   _____   50p + 70p   _____

75p + 80p   _____   75p + 75p   _____

Different coins, same amount

Make different amounts using different coins.
To make 75p using the fewest coins, you need a 50p, 20p and 5p. There are many other ways of making 75p.

1. Eddie bought a comic for 20p. He paid for it exactly with silver coins. There are several different ways he can do it. Can you find them all?

_____

_____

_____

_____

2. A drink costs 74p. What is the fewest number of coins I could use to pay?

_____

Find two other ways of paying.

_____

Which coins?

Look at the coins below. Using the fewest number of coins, make the total amount of money shown.

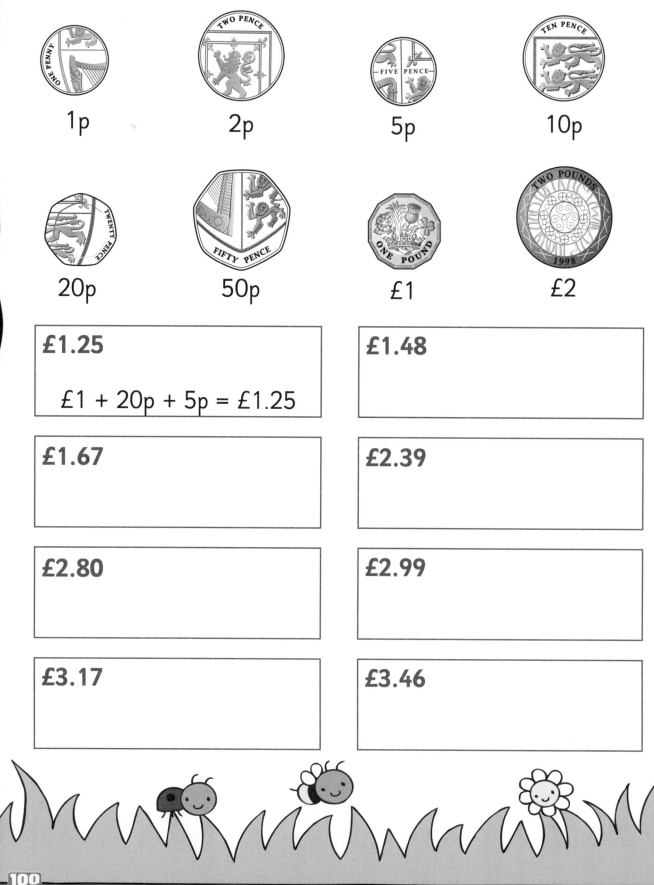

£1.25 £1 + 20p + 5p = £1.25	**£1.48**
£1.67	**£2.39**
£2.80	**£2.99**
£3.17	**£3.46**

Car boot sale

To find how much is spent, put the larger number in your head, count on the 10s and then add the 1s.
To work out the change, subtract the total from the money you started with.

Here are some items to buy. Answer the questions.

How much? _____

How much? _____

Pay for these items using silver coins only.

_____

Pay for these items with a £1 coin.

How much change will

you get? _____

You spend 96p altogether. What have you bought?

_____

_____

How many can you buy for £1?

_____

Describe me

Count the number of sides and corners of each shape.

- Does it have straight or curved sides?
- Is it symmetrical – can you fold it in half exactly?
- Is it a pentagon, a hexagon or an octagon? What is the same about the two octagons? What is different?

1. Sides: ____   Symmetrical: _____

   Corners: ____   Name: _____

2. Sides: ____   Symmetrical: _____

   Corners: ____   Name: _____

3. Sides: ____   Symmetrical: _____

   Corners: ____   Name: _____

4. Sides: ____   Symmetrical: _____

   Corners: ____   Name: _____

5. Sides: ____   Symmetrical: _____

   Corners: ____   Name: _____

Identifying 2D shapes

Hexagons have six straight sides.
Octagons have eight straight sides.

1. Tick the hexagons.

2. Circle the octagons.

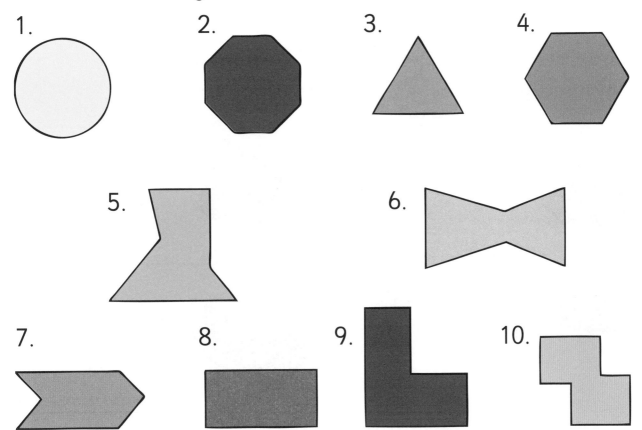

1.
2.
3.
4.
5.
6.
7.
8.
9.
10.

3. What are the names of the other shapes?

_____

_____

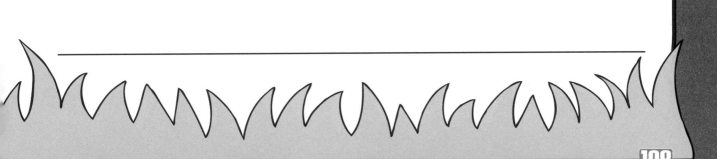

_____

Faces of 3D shapes

3D or solid shapes have faces which are 2D shapes. They could be squares, rectangles, circles, triangles, pentagons, hexagons and other shapes.

rectangle

Look at the 3D shapes. What 2D shape is the face coloured in dark blue? Write its name on the line.

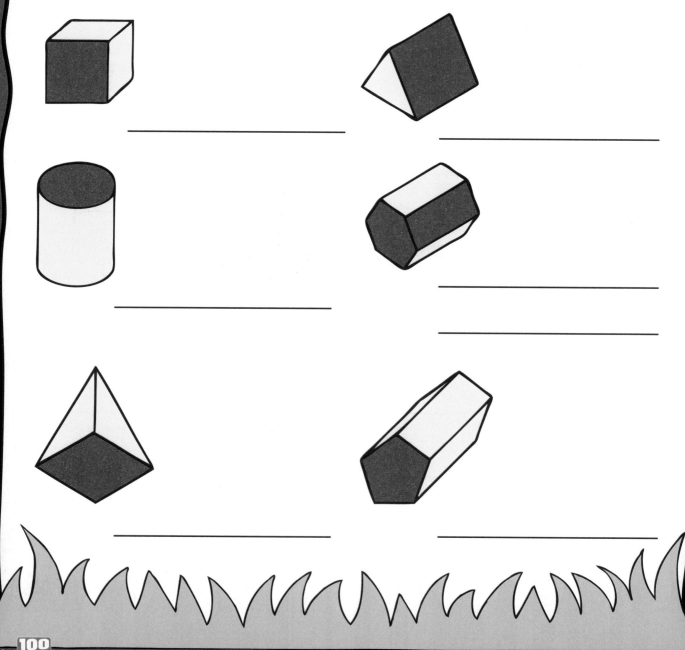

Drawing 2D shapes

Regular 2D shapes have equal length sides and angles. Joining the lines and dots with a ruler will help you learn how to draw 2D shapes.

Use a ruler to help you draw these shapes.

- Finish the shapes.
- Join the lines and join the dots.

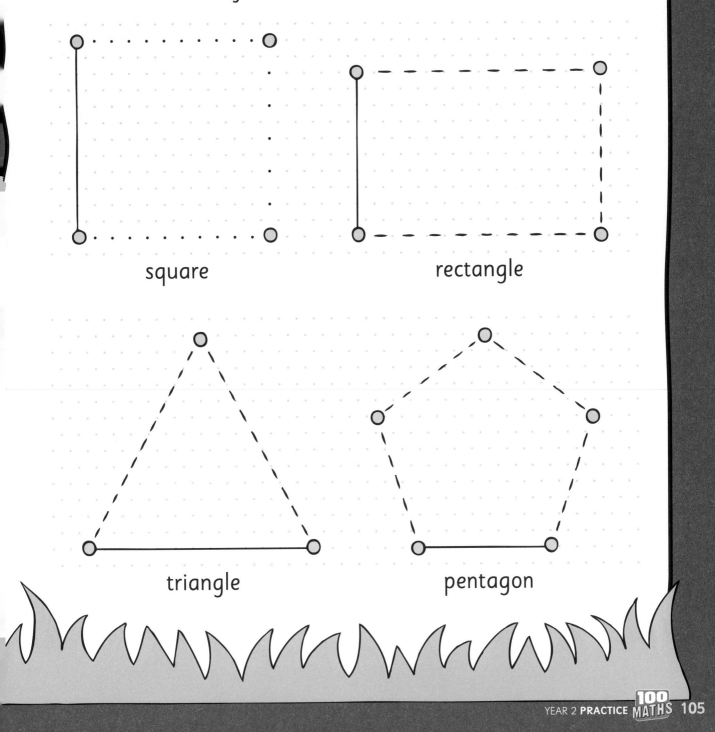

square

rectangle

triangle

pentagon

Describe 3D shapes

Write the correct shape name under each item. Draw a line to join each item to the correct shape description.

| one curved face
no edges or corners |

_____

| six square faces |

| one curved face
two circular faces |

_____

_____

| one curved face
one circular face |

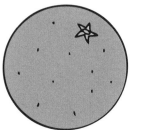

_____

| six rectangular
faces |

_____

Name the shape

Tip: If it has faces, it must be a 3D shape!

Draw a line from each clue to the correct shape.

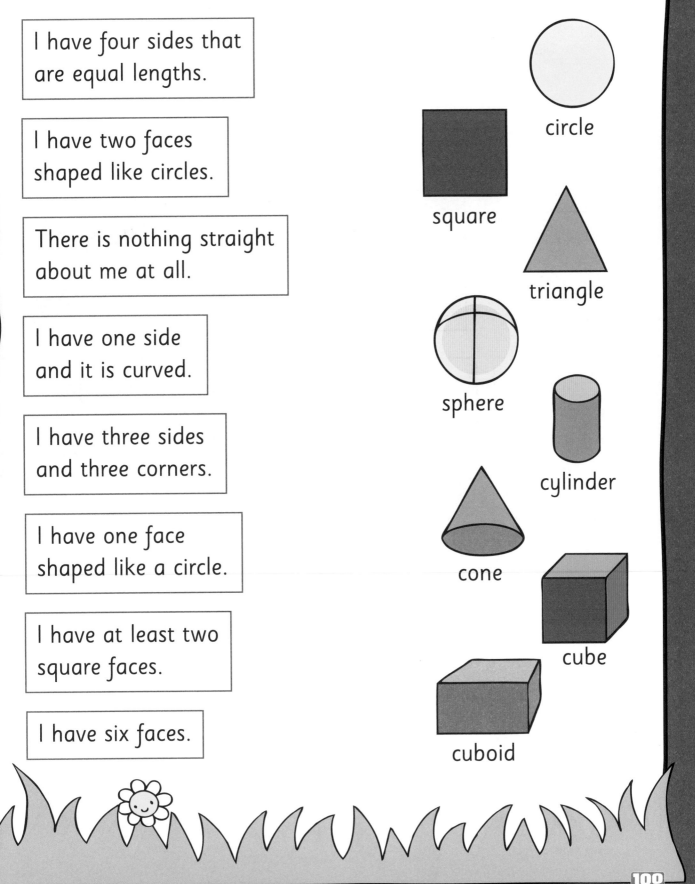

I have four sides that are equal lengths.

I have two faces shaped like circles.

There is nothing straight about me at all.

I have one side and it is curved.

I have three sides and three corners.

I have one face shaped like a circle.

I have at least two square faces.

I have six faces.

circle

square

triangle

sphere

cylinder

cone

cube

cuboid

Sorting 2D shapes

Draw a line from each shape to the correct shape name.

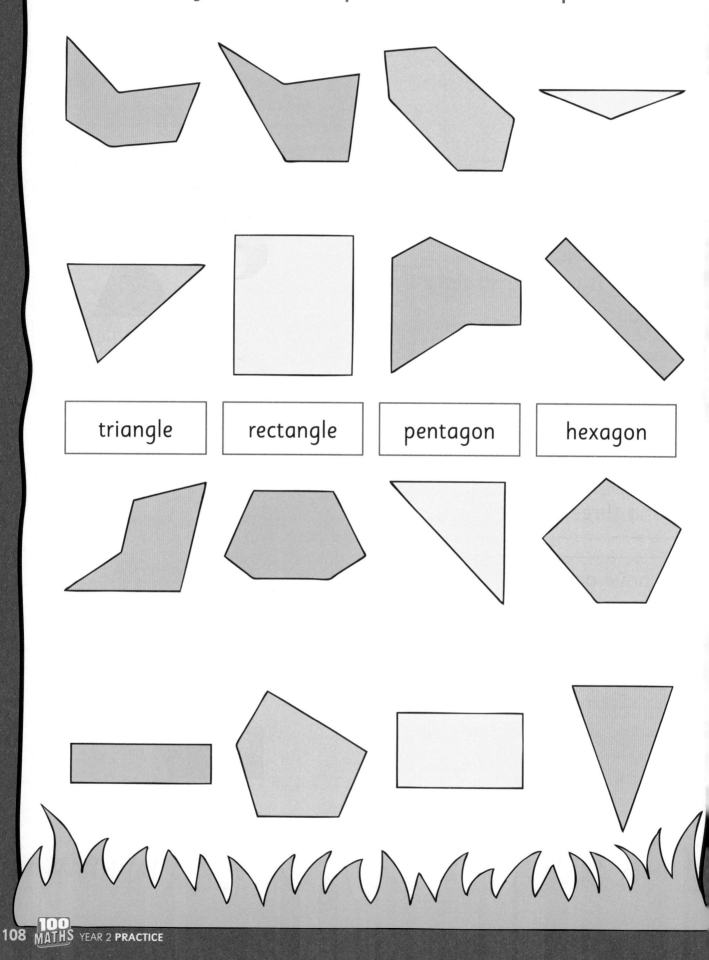

triangle   rectangle   pentagon   hexagon

Shape sorting diagram

A regular shape will have equal length sides and angles. It will help if you tick each shape as you sort it.

These are all shapes.

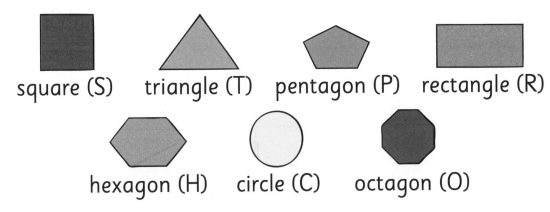

square (S) triangle (T) pentagon (P) rectangle (R)

hexagon (H) circle (C) octagon (O)

Write each shape's letter in the correct place on the diagram.

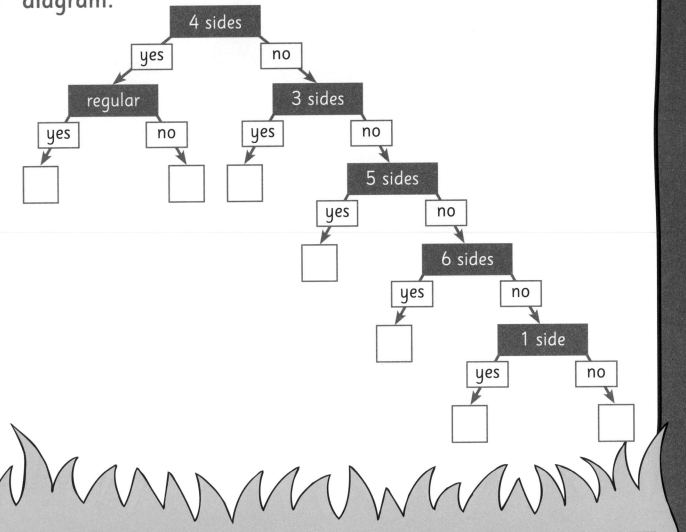

Sorting 3D shapes

Count the faces to help you sort these 3D shapes. Tick each shape as you sort it, so you don't miss any out.

1. Name each shape. Here are the words you will need.

| cone   cylinder   cube   sphere   pyramid   cuboid |

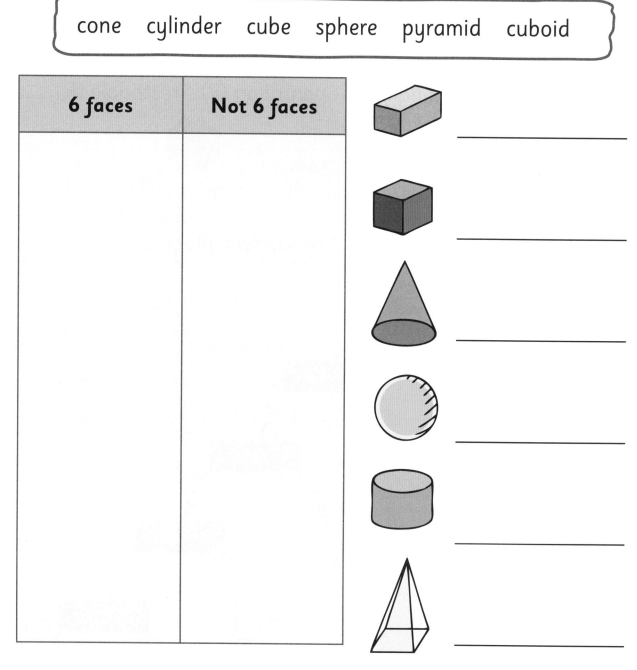

6 faces	Not 6 faces

2. Write the names to show where each 3D shape should go in the Carroll diagram.

Problems with shapes

1. How many triangles can you find in this pyramid?

2. Can you name this shape?
I am a 3D shape.
I have six edges.
I have four corners.
I have four triangular faces.
What is my name?

_____

Geometry: position and direction

Where am I heading?

If you turn **clockwise**, you turn in the same direction as clock hands. If you turn **anti-clockwise**, you turn in the opposite direction.

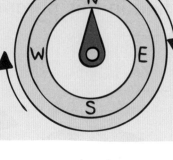

1. I am facing north. I take a quarter turn anti-clockwise. Which direction am I facing now?

    _____

2. I am facing south. I take a half turn clockwise. Which direction am I facing now?

    _____

3. I am facing east. I take a three-quarter turn anti-clockwise. Which direction am I facing now?

    _____

4. I am facing west. I take a three-quarter turn clockwise. Which direction am I facing now?

    _____

Directions

Program Robo-dog to rescue his owner. He must lead his owner to the forest entrance.

Starting at the forest entrance, give Robo-dog his commands to get back to his owner and then bring him back. Write down each command.

- Robo-dog can only move in straight lines.

- He cannot move through the trees.

- Explain carefully in what direction he should travel, such as 'Move forward two squares. Make a quarter turn clockwise.'

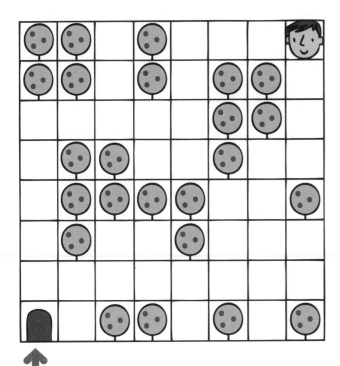

Forest entrance

_____

_____

_____

_____

_____

_____

_____

Patterns in shapes

A symmetrical pattern is the same on both sides.
Use a mirror down the line of symmetry to help you.

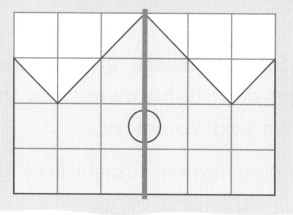

Complete the symmetrical pattern.

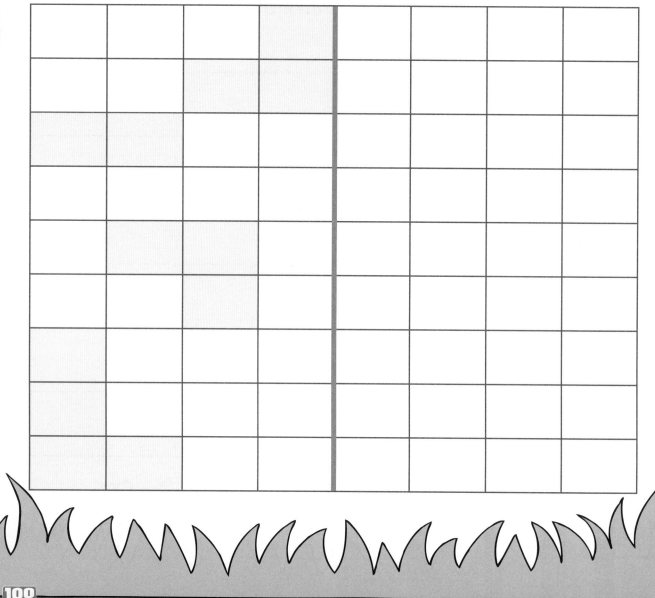

Follow the instructions to draw these shapes.

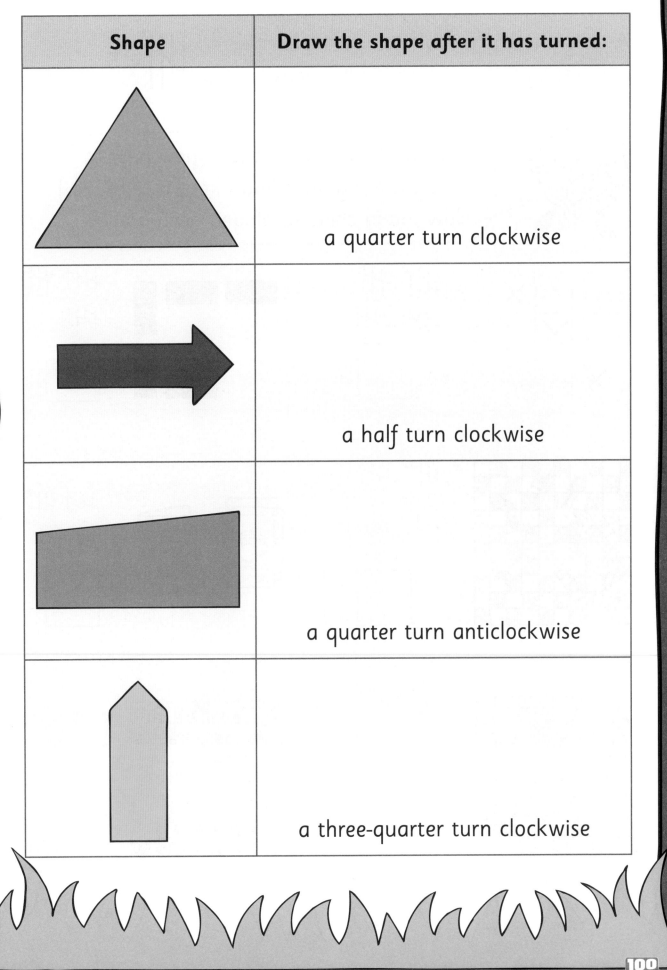

Shape	Draw the shape after it has turned:
	a quarter turn clockwise
	a half turn clockwise
	a quarter turn anticlockwise
	a three-quarter turn clockwise

Tally charts

A tally chart is a table which shows how many times something happens.

‖‖ = 5

I asked 20 children if they knew how to play these games and I kept a tally. How many children played each game?

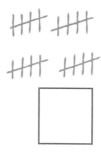

‖‖ ‖‖
‖‖ ‖‖

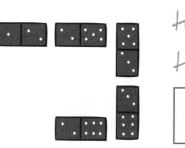

‖‖ ‖‖
‖‖

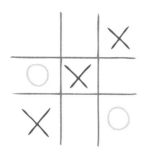

‖‖ ‖‖
|||

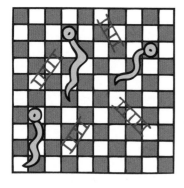

‖‖ ‖‖
‖‖ ||

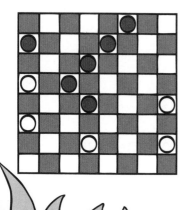

‖‖ ||

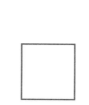

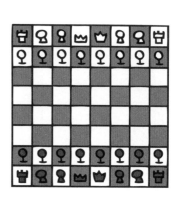

|||

Record the information from the games survey on this graph.

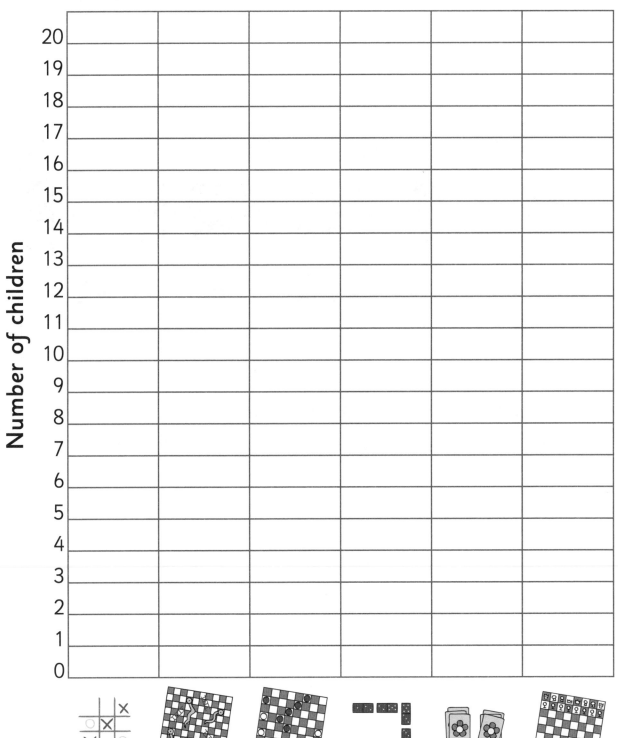

Number of children

Games

Drawing tallies

A tally is also a way of counting.

1. Tick all the children who are wearing bobble hats.

2. How many children are wearing bobble hats?

3. Complete the table by drawing tally marks to show how many children are wearing each of the items of clothing and then write the total.

Clothes	Tally	Total
Jumpers		
Scarves		
Bobble hats and jumpers		

Information in tables

Tables offer a clear and simple way to show information.

Favourite ice cream

	Vanilla	Chocolate	Raspberry
Number of children	6	9	12

This table shows that six children liked vanilla ice cream best. The most popular ice cream was raspberry.

Oak Class did a survey about favourite wild animals. This is what they found out:

- 7 children liked lions
- 8 children liked tigers
- 2 children liked crocodiles
- 5 children liked gorillas

1. Complete the table.

Favourite wild animals

	Lions	Tigers	Crocodiles	Gorillas
Number of children				

2. Which was the most popular wild animal? _____

3. Which was the least popular? _____

4. How many children were asked altogether? _____

Drawing a block graph

In a **block graph** one block represents one item of data.

Problem

I would like to order some paint for art, but I need you to help me decide which three colours to buy. I asked the class to tell me their favourite colours, and this is what they said:

> 2 liked black   3 liked orange   4 liked red
>
> 1 liked green   10 liked yellow   6 liked white

Draw the results as a block graph.

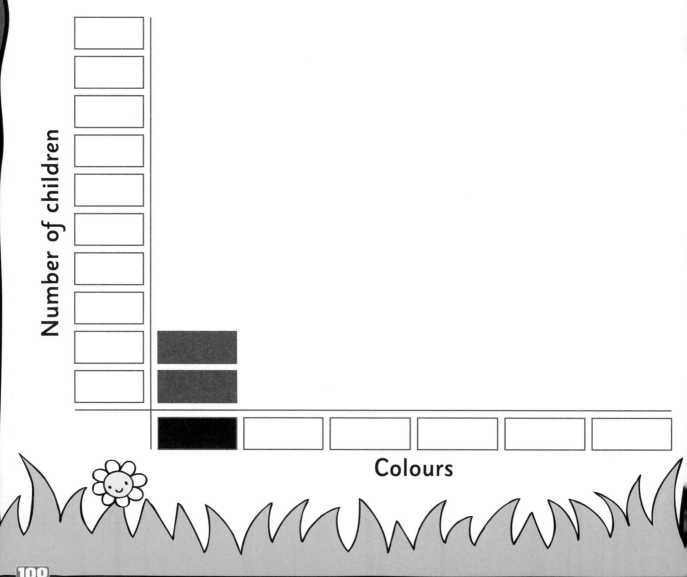

Take-away pictogram

A **pictogram** uses symbols to represent data. It must have a **key** to show how many items each symbol represents.

Josh did a survey to find out which was the most popular take-away food. Here are his results:

- 5 children liked pizza (p)
- 3 children liked burgers (b)
- 9 children like fish and chips (f and c)
- 4 children liked Chinese (Ch)
- 6 children liked curry (c)
- 2 children liked hotdogs (h)

Use this information to complete the pictogram below.

Key: ☺ = 1 child

Number of children						
10						
9						
8						
7						
6						
5	☺					
4	☺					
3	☺					
2	☺					
1	☺					
	p					

Take-away food

Favourite colours

☺ = 2 children.

This key shows that one symbol represents two children.

This pictogram shows a class's favourite colours.

Key: ☺ = 2 children

Number of children

1. Use the data to fill in the table.

	Red	Yellow	Blue	Brown	Orange
Number of children					

2. Write two sentences based on the data.

_____

_____

Faulty graph

Find seven faults with the graph shown below.

This pictogram shows our favourite farm animals.

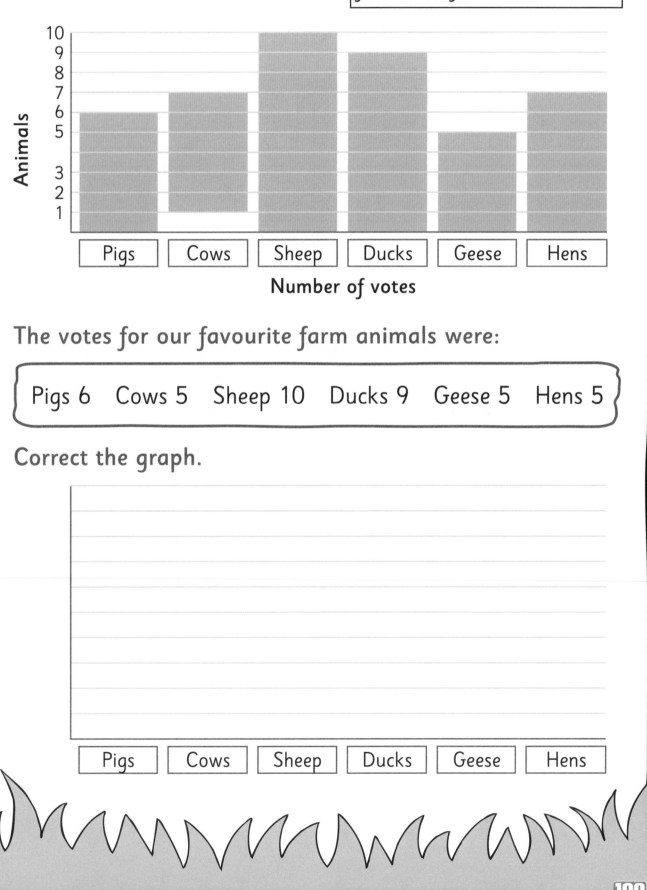

The votes for our favourite farm animals were:

Pigs 6   Cows 5   Sheep 10   Ducks 9   Geese 5   Hens 5

Correct the graph.

Carroll diagram

A Carroll diagram is used to sort data into groups.

Write these numbers in the correct places on the diagram below.

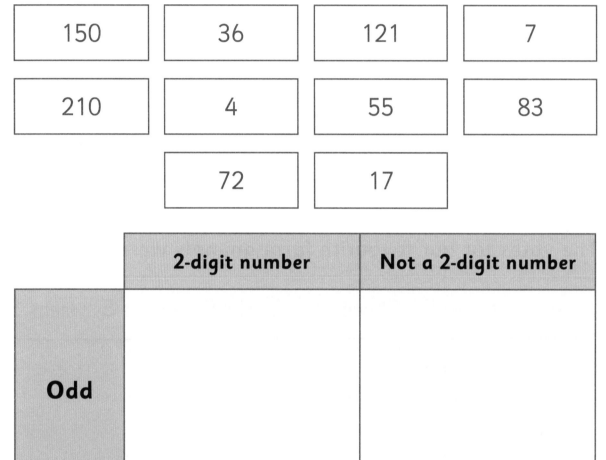

| 150 | 36 | 121 | 7 |

| 210 | 4 | 55 | 83 |

| 72 | 17 |

	2-digit number	Not a 2-digit number
Odd		
Not odd		

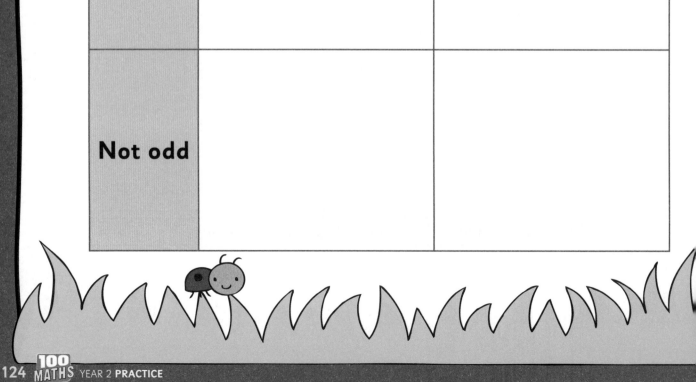

Sorting sports

Decide how to sort the sports into two groups.

1. Write the names of your two groups.

2. Draw a line from each sport to say which group it should go in.

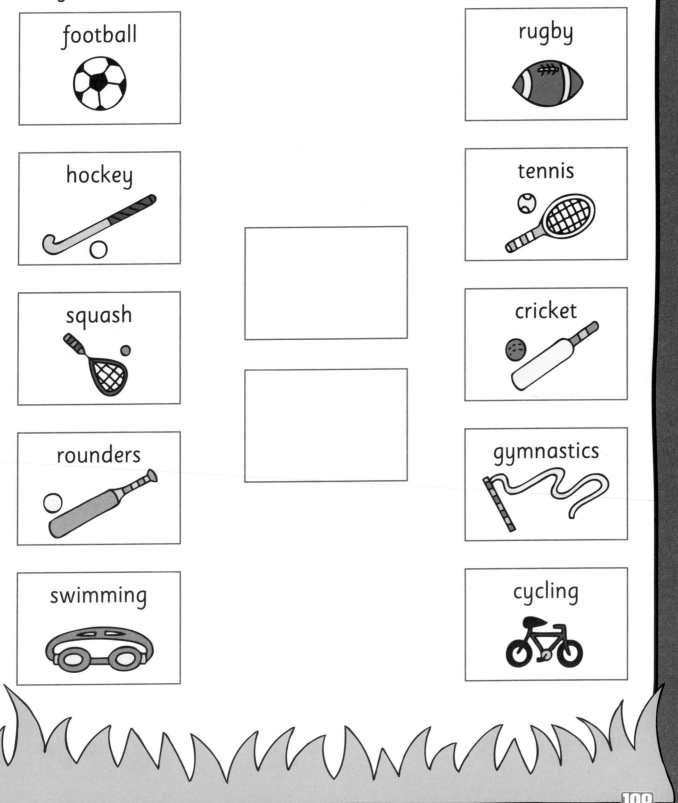

ress chart

king progress? Tick (✔) the flower boxes as you complete each section of the book.

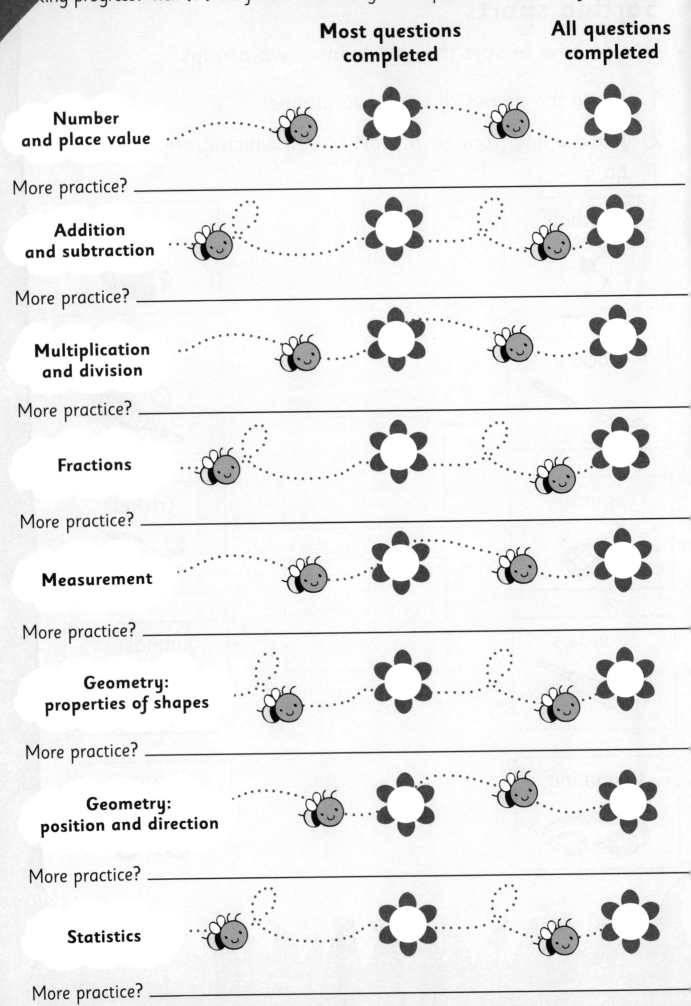

Most questions completed

All questions completed

Number and place value

More practice? _____

Addition and subtraction

More practice? _____

Multiplication and division

More practice? _____

Fractions

More practice? _____

Measurement

More practice? _____

Geometry: properties of shapes

More practice? _____

Geometry: position and direction

More practice? _____

Statistics

More practice? _____